MANAGING
BEYOND
THE ORDINARY

MANAGING
BEYOND
THEORDINARY

....

CHARLES H. KEPNER
HIROTSUGU IIKUBO

American Management Association

New York • Atlanta • Boston • Chicago • Kansas City • San Francisco • Washington, D.C.
Brussels • Mexico City • Tokyo • Toronto

Library of Congress Cataloging-in-Publication Data

Kepner, Charles Higgins
    Managing beyond the ordinary : using collaboration to solve
    problems, make decisions, and achieve extraordinary results /
    Charles H. Kepner, Hirotsugu Iikubo.
        p. cm.
    Includes bibliographical references (p.   ) and index.
    ISBN 0-8144-0336-0
    1. Management.   2. Problem solving.   I. Iikubo, Hirotsugu.
II. Title.
HD31.K4558   1996
658.4'03—dc20   96-8691
                                                               CIP

Printing number

10   9   8   7   6   5   4   3   2   1

Contents

Acknowledgments

Where do good ideas come from? Very few are created out of thin air. Most come from predecessors and coworkers, teachers, parents and other family members, from the culture within which we are born, and from experience, our day-to-day dealings with reality as we learn what works and what doesn't.

We want to acknowledge our debt to the thousands of people who have taught us all we know about collaboration and managing and to thank them for the associations we have had and for what we have been able to learn from them over the years. There are too many of them to name; in some cases, we never even knew their names. They know who they are, however, and we thank them. We hope we have represented their contributions fairly.

Two people we must name: our wives, Susan and Yoshiko. They have taught us more about collaborating and working together than anyone else. Without their participation, ideas, and support, we would have gone nowhere.

Introduction

This is how it really happened and why we wrote this book.

The top executives of the Alpha Corporation,* an auto manufacturing company, decided a few years ago that their auto assembly process needed to be more efficient. They identified certain welding operations as slow and difficult. "Let's automate these," they said. "That way we can reduce the number of people on the line and reduce costs." This was agreed to by the board of directors, and J. B. Whittaker, a high corporate official with a reputation for getting things done, was named to head the project.

Engineers were called in, studies were carried out, and robot welding machines were designed. This was all done off-premises so that the workers wouldn't feel threatened by the impending change. "We don't want to stir our people up," said Whittaker.

The robots were completed and tested by outside contractors. Then, at model changeover time, the lines were revamped and the robots brought in and installed. Many of the workers replaced by the robots were let go as redundant, with little advance notice. A few were transferred to lower-level jobs at reduced pay. The union immediately opposed the action, a strike was called, and the plant was shut down.

Millions of dollars of production were lost before it opened again. In the settlement, complex work rules were created that irritated both sides. Today, several years later, there is still distrust and animosity at that plant, and neither production nor quality has reached the level that management hoped for when the project was begun.

* All examples are real. The names of organizations and individuals are fictitious to protect everyone concerned.

Another auto company, the Beta Corporation, faced the same problem at about the same time. Its board decided that the assembly process should be made more efficient and named the plant manager to head the project. The board set specific goals for him: a 20 percent increase in production and a 10 percent decrease in labor cost. How he was to accomplish this was up to him.

The plant manager spent a lot of time thinking about his new task. He developed a list of objectives he would need to accomplish to reach his goal. As part of his strategy, he decided to add a number of robots. He called in his manufacturing manager and other key people, and together they identified areas where both quality and productivity could be improved and where the work caused excessive fatigue, slowed down the production flow, and increased the risk of poor worksmanship.

They then formed several groups, each of which included six experienced people who knew the operation firsthand, such as production specialists, machine operators, and foremen. These groups were assigned the task of thinking through how the targeted functions could be replaced by robots and what kind of robots these should be.

The plant manager provided the groups with time to work on the problem, discuss it, and generate and share ideas. Later, when the groups requested them, he provided materials and engineering assistance to create prototypes the group members thought could do the job. When these had been built and debugged, he brought in outside engineers and manufacturing people to translate the prototypes into finished hardware, with the group members acting as consultants and advisers. When the machines had been completed, he had the groups install, test, and finally operate them.

The robots worked better than expected, and the members of the groups that had designed them were proud and satisfied as a result. A plaque was placed on each machine noting the names of the workers who had contributed to its creation. Operators who were displaced by the robots were shifted to other jobs, and no one was fired or demoted. The robots were operated and maintained with care because they were the creative offspring of the people most concerned with getting the job done right. Improvements and adustments were made as the operator-designers worked with them and learned more about what they could do. Each robot soon acquired a pet name and was considered an almost-human member of the production team.

Who Did a Better Job?

We say the plant manager did a much better job of carrying out the task than Whittaker. Could anyone argue that J. B. was more efficient and produced better results than the manager? Whittaker didn't increase efficiency; he caused a strike and sharply decreased productivity. He didn't save money; he spent a lot and got little in return. Both men dealt with the same problem but took vastly different routes in trying to resolve it. Both worked hard at their projects, but the plant manager produced many times the results of J. B.

Whittaker focused on the task of installing robots, and nothing more. He took a narrow, outsider's view of the problem and paid attention primarily to numbers and symbols and mechanical things from which humanity had been removed. He didn't concern himself with other issues, human or otherwise.

He thought in terms of stations and functions. For Whittaker, people were interchangeable units, rather than an important part of the situation. He saw problems as purely objective arrangements of data about things, to be manipulated according to mathematical logic to achieve an efficient end result. He minimized the problem situation, choosing to perceive it as simple and skeletal in order to see it more clearly. He stripped the problem down to what he considered its essentials and focused all his attention on dealing with them.

Whittaker felt that it clarified the situation if one took out the people and dealt only with the machinery and the relationship of one piece of equipment to another. But to solve a problem of machines without considering people and other related aspects of the organization, as Whittaker did, is to solve an unreal, artificial problem that exists only in an abstract form in the mind. When the very real people in the rest of Whittaker's organization found out about Whittaker's plans, they were outraged at having been excluded from the process that led to those plans, and the "solution" fell apart.

Whittaker developed and put in robots, period. But his narrowly focused actions cost the organization millions in lost production, huge follow-on costs, and ill will and hostility that have persisted ever since. In addition, the robots never worked as well as expected. Whittaker never got the increased productivity he sought. He wasn't stupid. He just focused his energies on an excessively narrow view of the problem. He didn't consider the views of others but went ahead on the basis of his own inadequate conception of the situation.

At the Beta Corporation, the plant manager went at things in an entirely different way. He knew the local situation well, but he also knew he needed more information than he personally had, so he brought in other people who could help him see all the problems and implications attached to the project. He drew on the knowledge and expertise of his staff, who were involved and for whom the problem was important. He let them determine what the robots would do because they knew better than he did what would work and what wouldn't. The workers even built prototypes to prove that their ideas were sound. He then brought in technical people to refine the prototypes and turn them into hardware that would work.

The manager retained control of the project through his oversight, but he didn't fool himself into believing that he could mastermind the whole thing. He didn't "solve" a narrow problem himself; he *resolved* a broad problem situation that encompassed a number of related issues, through the help of his best workers and their knowledge. He didn't just "solve" the problem; he managed the successful completion of a series of tasks that resulted in the resolution of the entire situation.

Beyond the Ordinary

We say Whittaker did his job in an ordinary manner. He did what was required to install the robots and no more. He had a narrow focus that ignored and excluded related issues, and he paid a price in the problems that his organization suffered later on. At the conclusion of the project, he said, in effect, "This is the way we'll do it because I'm running this show, and I know best."

We contend that the plant manager went beyond the ordinary in his managing of the situation. He addressed a more inclusive view of the problem. He dealt with machines, people, and other issues raised by the introduction of robotics. He anticipated future problems and extended his understanding of the situation by drawing on the experience of those who knew the problem firsthand. He saw his job as manager in a different light and was far more successful as a result. He didn't work harder than if he'd just managed in the ordinary way; he managed smarter. He knew what to do in order to be maximally effective, and he did it. He didn't waste time on unimportant things. He got his staff to collaborate and to resolve the problem for him by completing the tasks he knew were necessary. At the conclusion of the project, he could say, "In our collective wisdom, this is the way we think it should be done." And he had all his workers solidly behind him, committed to making the project succeed.

Getting the Job Done

The job of a manager is to get things done. He or she has the organization's resources to work with—people, knowledge, facilities, money, all the things that make the organization go. The job of the manager is to use whatever of these are appropriate, in the most efficient way, to achieve the desired results. When something gets in the way of the organization, the manager's job is to get over or around or through the obstruction so that there can be progress toward the organization's destination. Whether something is wrong that has to be corrected, something is not as good as it could be and needs to be improved, or something is going to go wrong and needs to be prevented or avoided, problems are obstructions that impede progress. It is the manager's job to get them out of the way.

Some managers are better and get more done with less effort than others. They personally benefit from this, and so do their organizations. Their organizations grow faster, make more money, and are better places to work. Good management pays off. Resolving problems quickly and efficiently pays off. And so does anticipating and avoiding future problems.

The best managers get more of the things we value in this material world—money, respect, attention, promotions, opportunities—because they are worth more. They bring more gain and prevent more loss. Here we speak of managers as anyone who manages people and resources: executives, managers at all levels, and supervisors, whether in manufacturing, industry, service, or finance; scientists, academics, government and civilian workers; and all those who have responsibility for getting things done.

Yes, good managers get more of the good things than poor managers. Since all of us want to get our share of the good things, we need to ask, "Why are some managers better than others?" What do the best managers do that the others don't? How do they know where to put their energies to get the most done? How do they get others to collaborate with them and share their knowledge? And how can we learn to do likewise? This book is dedicated to exploring those questions and to finding practical answers you can use.

Modern management is complex and difficult. Ordinary effort is no longer enough. There aren't many isolated, simple problems that exist without accompanying issues nowadays, and there are guaranteed to be even fewer in the days that lie ahead. Going beyond the ordinary, accomplishing more than the minimum, getting others to cooperate in resolving problems, and drawing on the full knowledge and experience within the organization makes the difference between being a leader and being an also-ran in the competitive horse race we are all engaged in. It's as simple as that.

If you are an exceptional manager and go beyond the ordinary in what you do on the job, you may not gain much from the ideas we present here. But wouldn't it be nice if everyone else in your organization were as smart as you? You may have found it hard to tell others how to be as creative. You try to motivate them to work together and come up with better ideas; some respond, but others don't. They seem willing enough, but they don't know how to make it happen.

Collaboration Is the Key

There are answers to "How?" We want to examine what it means to manage beyond the ordinary—how and when to get your people to collaborate with you—in practical terms that you and your subordinates can use and apply. Talk is cheap, and preaching about good management is easy. But saying what to do, how to make it happen in the real world, is a bit more difficult.

This book is based on three assumptions:

1. Managers are people who are paid to resolve problem situations that impede the productivity and efficiency of their organizations. By "resolve," we mean to get rid of those problems totally and completely.
2. Managers can no longer do this by themselves but must draw on the best ideas and knowledge of their best-informed resource persons to create the actions that will completely resolve the problem situation.
3. There are a number of critical tasks to which collaboration contributes a great deal and that must be completed in order to achieve the resolution of a complex problem. Managers who recognize this and put their efforts where they will do the most good will manage significantly beyond the ordinary.

This much is clear. Managers need access to what others know in order to do their jobs, and they get that information by collaboration with their colleagues. The remainder of this book is devoted to how to do it, how to make it happen.

"But the corporate culture has to change before we can do that," some people say. "When the culture changes, we will be able to work more closely together." This may happen a long time from now, longer than you can afford to wait. Instead of hoping for the future, we will tell you how to bring it about today and how to change the future to your advantage.

You don't need to wait until your organizational world evolves. One person, collaborating and managing beyond the ordinary, can make a substantial difference, as our examples show. A number of people, working together, can make even more of a difference. An organizational unit, with its members all moving in the same direction, can make a huge difference. The tangible benefits of increased quality and satisfaction and accomplishment are waiting to be had. You can begin having them now. All you have to do is do it.

In this book we offer a lot of examples, many drawn from our professional practice, to show what managing beyond the ordinary through collaboration is. Few of the people involved or their organizations will be identified by name, because finger-pointing isn't necessary. Besides, you have plenty of your own examples that you can recall from experience. All of us have seen ordinary managers at work and others who went far beyond the ordinary. Think about the differences between the two, about how they related to you and the people around you. Then think how you can use those ideas tomorrow, adapted to your job.

It really is up to you. It's how you direct your effort as a manager, not how many hours you put in, that counts. It's the information and experience you draw on that makes the difference. Collaboration is fail-safe and easy. It's as simple as falling into a soft chair after a hard day's work. You can make it happen if you decide to do it.

SECTION ONE

An Overview of Collaborative Management

1

Managing Beyond the Ordinary: A Matter of Perspective

More than anything else, excellent management—managing beyond the ordinary—is a matter of perspective. And clearly, some managers are more effective than others. The effective ones don't work any harder than those who aren't; they just see the task of managing in a different way. They recognize when a problem is complex and their information inadequate and recognize when they need to know more than they do and reach out to their people for help. As a result, they end up learning things they didn't know and doing things other managers do not, and they avoid doing a lot of things that less effective managers do. They don't waste time. They go to the heart of the matter and find out and do the right things from the beginning.

That doesn't mean they know all the answers, what caused the problem situation and what to do about it. It does mean that they know what they will have to do to find all the answers. They know where they are going in terms of problem-resolving procedures. They know that if they ask the right questions of the right people, the answers they need will appear. They identify the important dimensions of the situation and don't waste time around its edges.

Some look at the job of managing as a narrow activity, just "selling the product" and "getting the iron out the door." This leads them into short-term, highly specific decisions as they deal with problems they have defined in a narrow and specific way. The more-effective managers look at the job broadly and in greater depth. They see problems as series of related issues that others may know more about than they do. They consider their long-term goals and pay attention to human relationships. They draw on the experience and judgment of their best-informed co-workers to help them determine what is truly important. Then they make short- and long-term decisions and create a more stable and prosperous business environment for everyone as a result.

THE DANGERS OF A NARROW FOCUS

Sam Bartell was both chief executive officer and chairman of Bartell Computer Services, which supplied computer and financial training, systems, and services to a wide range of clients. Bartell Computer was considered a leader in its field and was known for the quality of its work, but in time it found its service getting harder to sell.

The company's field representatives complained that their service was no longer seen by the public as superior, as it once had been. Other organizations were offering similar services at lower cost, with added new features. Yet Bartell Computer hadn't changed or improved its product much in years. The vice president of sales, Marie Davis, and the VP of research and development, Joe Crawford, were painfully aware of this.

At one board meeting, where Sam Bartell was complaining about failure to meet projected revenues, Crawford said, "Our service is becoming obsolete. We've got to make improvements to meet the modern needs of our clients." Davis strongly agreed, as did a third VP. Changes and improvements had to be made, no question about it.

Bartell was furious at this and attacked the three VPs personally. "Our product is not obsolete! There's nothing wrong with it! You just aren't selling hard enough!" He said that there was no need for a "panic to change" and argued that "what we have to do is make our numbers." After ranting for a few minutes more, Bartell ordered some cosmetic changes for the sales organization, and nothing was done to improve the service offered their clients.

Davis and Crawford were seated at the table across from each other. Their eyes went up to the blank walls of the conference room, and Davis was silent for the rest of the meeting. The outside board members agreed with Bartell. The third VP quickly dropped the idea of making any changes and also agreed with Bartell.

The immediate, narrow problem was "making the numbers," meeting the monthly revenue targets. Nothing else mattered. There were no other problems or issues to be dealt with. That was it. Bartell was "number-driven," rather than motivated by concern for the clients or for the long-term health of the organization. If the horse didn't run fast enough, the answer was to beat it harder! The fact that the horse hadn't been fed well and was getting old was beside the point. The solution was to hire a jockey with more muscle!

This is in fact what happened. The next week Marie Davis, a good person who had done everything possible to increase revenue to little avail, resigned. The issues of obsolescence were not being addressed, and she knew she couldn't achieve a turnaround without a better product. Two years later, after exhausting its full line of credit, borrowing on the life insurance policies of its officers, and going through a succession of new sales VPs, the organization began to improve its product. In time, it became profitable again. But it was years before it recovered the ground it had lost. Sam Bartell blamed it all on unfortunate circumstances and a weak economy.

Sam Bartell managed in an ordinary, uninspired way. He believed, "If it ain't broke, don't fix it." As long as anybody bought the service at all, it must be all right. He also believed that nobody could understand the product and the needs of the organization as well as he could. Wasn't he the CEO and chairman? He listened to the people who told him what he wanted to hear, and there were plenty of those around. He cut off anyone who had different views. So sell harder! Have more sales meetings! Beat that horse, and he'll run like a deer again! Bartell worked long hours and spent a lot of energy doing things that didn't help resolve the problem of low revenues. Turnover in his organization climbed higher. Sam Bartell was not a much-loved chief executive.

Bartell's style cannot in any way be seen as effective management. Had Bartell looked beyond the end of his nose, he could not have helped questioning whether there was a problem with the product. Had he asked, he could have gotten the honest, best ideas of his field representatives, those who knew the product and the client needs best. He could have gotten the same information from his customers. He could have seen the big picture clearly, had he not assumed that he already knew everything. He would not, could not have jumped to the conclusions that he did without finding out what was really going on. He had opportunities to find out what he needed to know, but he passed them up. And he probably would have worked less hard doing a good job than he did doing a lousy one.

As far as Bartell was concerned, there were no other issues involved with the shortfalls in revenue. Why should he ask questions of anyone? He knew the answers: People were lazy and needed to sell harder. And there wasn't anything wrong with his organization. Everything was all right except for the lack of effort the people in sales were putting out. He didn't consider the long-term strategies or purpose of his organization beyond "meeting the numbers." He focused his attention solely on the problem of meeting the unrealistic targets he had set, and he let the rest go.

Sam often talked about goals, long-term strategy, and the importance of thinking ahead. Every year he had a session with his top managers at which statements of corporate purpose were drawn up in detail, but he never referred to these statements in day-to-day decision making. Instead, he ignored all the information that was readily available to him and acted alone on the basis of his own narrow, incomplete perception of the problem at hand. The ultimate irony in this, of course, is that Bartell Computer Services sold and installed networks for its clients so that people could communicate and share ideas. He ignored the opportunities he had for collaboration and almost ruined his organization. By expanding his understanding of the problem and asking others to contribute what they knew, Bartell could have saved millions of dollars. But since the wheels had not yet fallen off his organization, he decided there was no sense fixing anything.

Bartell was supported in this folly by the sycophants around him who were more interested in keeping him happy than in the good of the company. After the crisis had been weathered, his do-nothing board voted him a six-figure special bonus for having "saved" the company. Joe Crawford quit in disgust.

The Ordinary Manager

Was Bartell Computer an isolated, unusual case? Unfortunately, no. We have seen dozens like it. Tough, thick-skinned, "practical" managers feel most comfortable with the status quo as long as it seems to be working. But that's a risky proposition. It says, "Be totally reactive. Wait until disaster strikes before you do anything." It's the best sure-fire recipe imaginable for a run-down, marginal, crisis-ridden, hopeless operation. The best it can ever achieve is more of the same, with little possibility for improvement. The worst it can lead to is collapse and a slide into oblivion that no one can fix.

Yet passivity is the byword of the ordinary manager. Don't ask questions and do the minimum to keep things going; don't stretch yourself to do anything extra and don't look for trouble. When trouble finally strikes, look surprised. Blame someone lower in the hierarchy; then try to fix things with a dramatic flourish and a great show of determination so that people will think you know what you're doing. That's the way the ordinary manager does it, and it's not very effective.

There are a lot of ordinary managers around. When something goes wrong, they rush in to fix it. They are great problem solvers, and they get a lot of practice. They see themselves as invaluable to the organization, and they believe the company couldn't get along without them. Who would handle all the problems if they weren't on hand?

Not all are as bad as Sam Bartell. Many are shortsighted, but they survive and do many things fairly well. They aren't in a position to cause a total collapse of the organization, but they drain its effectiveness. Their organizations are never as profitable and as successful as they might be. Occasionally, some of them wonder why. Their subordinates could tell them, but no one ever asks what they think about anything. And so it goes, the ordinary manager within the ordinary organization, achieving ordinary results.

The Manager's Job

As has already been stated, the manager's job is to get things done, using whatever resources are available. The manager is given responsibilities that need to be carried out as well as possible so that the organization can remain competitive.

But bad things continually happen, things go wrong, and there are barriers to carrying out those responsibilities. Then the manager has to get his or her subordinates to repair and fix what broke down, improve things that aren't as good as they might be, correct other things that aren't moving in the right direction, and avoid troubles that lie ahead. To do that, the manager has to know what's happening, both in the organization and in the world beyond.

Some say the manager's job is to have vision and not to "get bogged down in problems." "Aim high and do it better than it ever has been done before!" We say vision is tremendously important, and bigger and better should be the goal of every manager. But we question whether you can have vision for the future if you don't know what the present problems are and whether you can really get to those better things if you don't remove or get around the barriers that lie in the way. Vision isn't necessarily bulldozing the landscape clean to start over in an entirely new direction. It is recognizing what needs to be done, what needs to be improved, and then organizing resources and getting it done.

The Plane Truth—A Tale of Two Airports

Stapleton, the old airport serving Denver, Colorado, had only two runways, and in periods of bad weather, only one runway could be used at a time because of the limitations of the existing landing system. There were many ways the old airport could have been expanded and made better at a modest cost. But because Denver boosters wanted a "visionary airport . . . one of the biggest and most technologically advanced in the world," they rejected the old ideas about what an airport should be and designed a futuristic marvel, the Denver International Airport, with a computerized baggage system and all sorts of whiz-bang innovations. Unfortunately, these high-tech gizmos didn't work when the airport was supposed to open. The futuristic baggage system shredded suitcases instead of delivering them at the right place on time, and there were a lot of other problems. The airport finally opened on February 28, 1995, sixteen months late and $3.2 billion over budget.

At about the same time, the Tokyo International Airport, the new Haneda, was completed on filled land in Tokyo Bay. Japanese developers took the best ideas about airport design from around the world, then made improvements wherever they found shortcomings. They asked the people who knew what the problems were about how to correct them. They didn't set out to create a futuristic vision of what an airport should be but took the very best now in existence and made it better. They resolved thousands of big, medium-size, and little problems and created what is perhaps the best airport in the world—which turns out to be a new vision of what an airport can be. And they did it on schedule and on budget. The airport is spotless, elegant, and incredibly efficient.

Planners of the Denver airport ignored the known problems and aimed at creating a traveler's paradise where there would be no problems. Unfortunately, they created new problems that had never existed before, so airlines using the new terminal have been forced to charge passengers an extra fee to defray their added cost. The Haneda planners identified all the problems they could find and resolved them, one by one. They anticipated what might go wrong and took steps to see that it didn't. And they created an airport where the baggage is there waiting for its owners, without a nick or dent, because they asked the baggage handlers how to improve the baggage system. Like having a vision, seeking collaboration in the resolution of problems is essential.

Problems are things that aren't right and that concern people to the extent they want to make them better. Problems are trouble spots that have to be resolved if there is to be any prog-ress; they hold organizations and people back, cost money, and reduce quality. Improvement starts with the recognition that a problem exists; otherwise, how could anyone know that there is a need for improvement? A manager is the person who marshals resources to solve the problem—either in an ordinary, pedes-trian way or in a way that goes beyond the ordinary.

Something that is ordinary is not very good, barely accept-able. An ordinary coat is a coat, but that's about all. An ordinary movie is so-so, one you wouldn't recommend to a friend. An ordinary meal fills the belly but is forgotten an hour later, except for the heartburn. An ordinary manager gets the minimum job done, but not much more.

Ordinary organizations, directed by ordinary managers, drag down the economy. They make big plans and hire a lot of people, then find things didn't work out the way they planned and have to fire them. They call this "constructive downsizing." They go through cycles of expansion and contraction, blaming the ups and downs on economic trends. They are experts in short-term thinking. They take shortcuts, compromise quality, and alienate their customers. They are highly active and go through a lot of motions but make little forward progress.

But some manage beyond the ordinary. They do more of the right things without working any harder because they make use of what their colleagues know. Life runs smoothly in their organizations, and they contribute more to profit because they don't waste time and effort in nonproductive activities. Their ideas are good, and their decisions are part of an overall plan, not disjointed events unconnected to anything else. People grow within their organizations and are appreciated for the ideas they contribute. What business needs is more people who know how to collaborate with others and manage beyond the ordinary.

Managing beyond the ordinary is going beyond the bare minimum through collaboration. It is doing what needs to be done plus what *ought* to be done to make things as good as pos-sible, and doing these things by the best means known. It is recognizing the opportunity to do more and doing it. It is doing for management what has so successfully been done for quality: *getting it right the first time.*

How do people manage beyond the ordinary? They develop a humble perspective. The don't assume they know it all. They seek out the best ideas from people who have special skills and knowledge and integrate this information to create a complete resolution to the problem. Managing this way comes easily to some people and must be learned by others. But anyone can manage beyond the ordinary if he or she tries.

The Focus of Collaboration

Collaboration is a process in which two or more individuals with complementary knowledge and skills focus on a common problem or issue and work together to create a resolution neither of them could have achieved alone. They are *thinking together* as if they had become a single mind, rather than just cooperating or working together. They are putting their heads together and pooling their ideas to achieve a shared understanding of a problem and how they can best resolve it.[1]

People need to focus on the same thing in order to think together. They can then contribute facts, judgments, experiences, opinions, and innovative ideas and combine these to create a new conception that none of the individuals would have come up with alone. That is collaboration: focusing on a single subject, thinking together, and then integrating the best of those thoughts into a new entity. Otherwise, collaboration can't occur, and they will have a rambling discussion at best.

What do you and your colleagues focus on when you set out to resolve a problem through collaboration? You must identify a problem, the area of concern, and focus your attention on that. To resolve that problem completely, there are ten critical tasks that must be completed. These ten tasks are at the heart of this book. You focus on each one in turn as you work your way through to a resolution. Each begs for the best ideas available. With these tasks as a focus, you and your people can think together and share your ideas to create a better way of dealing with the situation than any of you could have achieved alone.

The Ten Critical Tasks

1. *To understand the situation fully and know what is going on.* You can't deal with any situation until you have a clear grasp of what is happening.
2. *To clarify the purpose you and your colleagues are trying to serve by whatever actions you are considering.* You can't determine how to get somewhere until you are clear on where you are going.
3. *To find out what you and your colleagues need to know to resolve the problem and who has that information.* You can't decide whom to question or what questions to ask until you know what it is you want to find out.
4. *To get the complete story about the problem.* You and your co-workers can't develop more than a partial resolution if you have only part of the picture.
5. *To know what the cause of the problem is and to be able to prove it.* You and your colleagues can't be sure how to correct something if you don't know how it happened in the first place.
6. *To determine what specifically needs to be accomplished to resolve the problem.* You and your colleagues can't know which actions to take until you all know what has to be done.
7. *To find the best possible actions to achieve your purpose.* You and your colleagues can't be sure that your resolution is the best it can be until you have looked at all the possibilities open to you and evaluated which can accomplish your purpose most efficiently.
8. *To put the best actions you and your co-workers can find into a practical program that can be implemented.* You haven't come to a resolution until you have integrated your actions into a feasible sequence that will work.
9. *To fine-tune your plan until it is as good as it can possibly be.* You and your co-workers aren't finished with your plan until you have accomplished what you set out to do and then removed whatever barriers to its success you can foresee.
10. *To present your plan to those who must approve it in such a*

clear and logical way that they understand and accept it. You and your co-workers can't claim to have resolved your problem until the resolution is agreed to and put into effect.

Ten tasks, ten points at which your co-workers can focus their knowledge and experience to give you the benefit of what they have learned over the years. If you think together, you can all extend your understanding of what is going on. Your co-workers know things about the situation that you don't and can help you determine who should be involved in the resolution. They will have insight into the details of the problem and what might have caused it. They can help you understand what needs to be improved and the best ways of getting it done. Together, you can devise a plan of action that will work and determine how to present it so that others can also understand and accept it. Together, you can reach a resolution that would be beyond the grasp of any of you individually.

What if Sam Bartell had asked the people who really knew about sales in the field to focus with him on these ten tasks? He would have developed an entirely different picture of what ailed his company. He would have listened to his VPs and learned that the company's service was in fact going out of date. And he could have discovered how to cure his organization's troubles. He could have saved millions and some good careers. His colleagues knew things he didn't and would have been proud to share their ideas with him. But they never had a chance, because Bartell knew all the answers and so failed his organization and himself most of all.

Summary

The job of a manager is to get things done, using the resources available in the best, most efficient way possible. The most valuable resources a manager has to draw on are the minds and ideas of his or her colleagues. To take advantage of this fund of talent, the manager and they must think together, as if they had become a single mind, focused on the same aspect of the problem at the same time. The necessary ten tasks that must be completed in order to resolve a problem completely are the same points on which they can most productively focus and collaborate.

Managing beyond the ordinary is a matter of perspective. It requires seeing the ideal resolution of a complex problem as the result of a collaboration between you and your best-informed people as you *think together* through a series of specific tasks. If you all complete all of the tasks together, you will have reached the best possible resolution of the situation, given the information available.

That's all there is to it. It's nothing mysterious or earth-shaking. It's using the intelligence and experience of your colleagues in a disciplined manner to find a better way. Anyone can do it.

Note

1. Michael Schrage, *Shared Minds* (New York: Random House, 1990).

2

Collaboration and Management Thinking

The manager's job is to get things done and to use the resources available to remove barriers that stand in the way of achieving the company's goals. Doing this successfully requires a high level of thinking. Good thinking and good ideas produce good management.

Management thinking is no different from any other kind of thinking. It is normal human thought, applied to the complex problems and issues of management. The same head, brain, and memory for experience are put to work at this job as for any other nonmanagement mental undertaking—except that management is different in scope and detail from almost any other human activity. Few fields of endeavor demand so much of a person. Consider what a manager has to deal with:

- Objects and conditions, systems and organizations
- People and their perceptions, aspirations, fears and motivations, performance and behaviors
- Interrelationships among objects, people, and past, present, and future systems
- Matters of value and importance, right and wrong, goals, objectives, and standards
- The act of thinking itself—how to do it better, how to draw out the thinking of others and put ideas together to form new conceptions
- Predictions about the future—how to avoid future trouble

and take advantage of opportunities, how to plan and create a better tomorrow
- Questions and needs for which there are no present answers, abstracts for which there are no concrete expres-
sions

And much, much more. . . .

Few tasks in management are simple and isolated. If a management problem looks simple and isolated, it's possible that
you don't understand the situation or that it has been artificially
simplified and its true dimensions distorted. Real management
situations consist of a mix of details, problems, and issues that
threaten those who have responsibility for producing quality results.

This complexity means that every problem and issue is
linked to other aspects of the organization, creating new issues
that have to be understood and dealt with if the problem is to be
fully resolved, controlled, or managed. The most serious errors
of management come when managers ignore or don't appreciate
this interconnectedness and treat complex situations as if they
were simple. They may then underestimate their need for information and settle for only half the story, leading to flawed decisions and halfway solutions. They then run the risk of getting
lost in the details and applying simple thinking to complex situations, while believing that they have done their job.

It is optimistic to assume that we can apply our relaxed
thinking habits to the complexities of management and have
them succeed. Management calls for heavy-duty thinking, the
best we can produce. Managers need all the mental horsepower
they can command, both theirs and their co-workers', to deal
with the flood of problems and issues they face every day.

Individual Styles of Thinking

In spite of the fact that we all have roughly the same cranial
equipment, we have each developed our own slightly different
ways of using it. We have come by our individual ways natu-

rally; they derive partly from heredity and partly from our experiences of growing up among other people.

As we become specialized in our favorite style of thinking, we may overlook other ways. Some of us favor hard-nosed observations and the use of data in our thinking and end up engineers and scientists. Others think more in terms of experiences and appearances, feelings and interrelationships, and engage in the softer sciences or provide services or sell things. Still others of us think along the lines of intangible and aesthetic concerns and become artists and writers. In spite of the fact that we are each capable of all modes of thought, we tend to rely upon a particular one; the more overloaded we are, the more we depend on our favorite way of thinking.

We carry these predilections into the field of management, where we are overloaded and challenged every day. As managers, we need to think about a wide range of topics—people, what is most important, the future—all at the same time. We naturally depend on our most trusted thinking mode, whether it is appropriate to the matter at hand or not, and use it on everything because we know it has worked for us in the past. Someone once said, "To one who has only a hammer, everything else is a nail." The same thing applies to the ways we choose to think.

If we become too analytical and dedicated to the facts before us, we will demand only hard and specific data and ignore everything else. In so doing, we may miss a lot of information that might be important. If we depend on past experience and how we feel about things, we may accept as true some propositions that later turn out to be questionable. Too much reliance on one mode can blind us to useful information that is coming through another channel or from other sources, leading us into wrong decisions.

THE CATASTROPHIC FAILURE OF THE SPACE SHUTTLE *CHALLENGER* ON JANUARY 28, 1986

More than a dozen engineers of the Morton Thiokol Corporation, manufacturer of the shuttle's solid rocket boosters, were in unanimous agreement that it was too cold that morning to launch.

There was a heavy accumulation of ice on the pad with a sharp breeze blowing. The plastic O-rings would be too stiff to seal the joints in the rocket body. On the basis of their experience and their intuition, the engineers recommended that the launch be delayed until it became warmer.

The NASA executives, also engineers, were faced with intense pressures to get the shuttle off that morning. Their frustration was given voice when one of them said, "My God, Thiokol, when do you want me to launch—next April?" They rejected the verbal recommendations of the people who knew the most about the O-rings and demanded facts and figures as evidence. But Thiokol's engineers had no experimental laboratory data. Their judgment told them it was too cold, but they couldn't produce a single graph or table of measurements to defend their position. So the launch went forward, in spite of their strong convictions, and seventy-three seconds into the flight, the O-rings failed, the shuttle blew up, and seven people died.

Both sides were at fault in this tragedy. The Thiokol engineers' intuitions were based on years of firsthand experience and intimate knowledge of the O-rings. Their conclusions were as correct as any that could have come out of the laboratory with volumes of experimental findings to back them up, but they didn't go further to prove in a rational way that their intuitions were correct. The NASA people were correct in being skeptical and wanting solid data, but they didn't do anything to understand and or try to confirm the valid concerns raised by the Thiokol engineers. It was as though the parties spoke different languages, each incomprehensible to the other, with no way to span the gap between them. They had the very best communication equipment that money could buy, but they didn't use it to broaden and combine the information they had. Instead, they argued one side against the other, the lack of precise engineering data pitted against judgment based on experience.

It was up to Dr. Richard Feynman, a Nobel prize winner and member of the presidential commission appointed to investigate the accident, to bridge the gap between the two modes of thinking. He took a piece of the plastic O-ring material and stuck it in a glass of ice water, then showed how stiff it had become from the cold. He then pointed out that it had been ten degrees colder on the pad at the time of the launch. From that simple demonstration, it was obvious that cold had stiffened the plastic material to the point that it could no longer seal the rocket joints. Feynman had proven the intuitions of the Thiokol engineers to be correct.[1] The cause of the accident became inarguable from that point forward.

The real tragedy lay in the unwillingness of the two parties to reconcile the differences between "We think it is too cold" and "Where are your data?" Feynman did it by sticking a piece of O-ring material into a glass of ice water. Thiokol could have done the same thing in a few minutes, putting a piece of the material in a lab freezer and dropping its temperature down to the 25° F. reading observed on the pad, and looking at the results. NASA could have done the same thing to see if there was any merit in Thiokol's claim. In either case, the result would have been enough to postpone the launch. Instead, they chose to stick with their single-track modes of thought and argue at length about who was right—and in the process killed seven people.

There should be no competition between ways of thinking. All ways are good and have their place; all can produce valuable ideas. Management requires the best thinking available from everyone involved—and that means thinking done in all modes.

The different modes of thinking do have their own built-in limitations. If you choose to draw heavily upon intuition and experience, your evidence will be vulnerable to error, and you must be prepared to verify your conclusions with direct observation or experiment. On the other hand, if you rely heavily on numbers and data, you will be using only a portion of what is known and available, and you will have to search beyond those facts for what others have learned from experience.

There must be a balance between the hard-nosed, "show me your evidence" approach, and the reasonable use of experience, informed judgment, gut feelings, and accumulated wisdom. Both are valid sources of information, but the limitations of each should be understood. We suggest that the "natural-born manager" is the person who, by hard lessons along the way, has learned how to achieve that balance and to use all modes all the time. Every manager has an obligation to use all available modes of thinking to reach the best resolution possible for every problem encountered.

Modes of Management Thinking

There are three distinct modes or different ways of management thinking, and managers need to use all three in combination. They must also understand the strengths of each mode and how and when to use it, how to integrate the products of each mode into a single body of information they can trust, and, most of all, how to draw on each mode for the best it can offer.

Psychologists would argue with our comments about the modes of thinking and see them as too simple. We offer them only as descriptive categories for practical use, not as theoretical entities. They are intended as tools to help us understand what goes on inside our heads when we decide how to deal with a problem.

First, we need to define what we mean by "thinking." We see thinking as the process of mentally manipulating units of information to produce a conclusion that we consider valid and true. What goes on at the level of neuron interaction is beyond our understanding and is not our concern here. How information is manipulated so that the neurons can function at their best, on the other hand, should interest us a great deal, because we can do something about that. If we can find the best way to organize and feed data to the brain, it can do more and better work for us, and our thinking will improve.

The three modes we have identified have to do with how information is acquired and used in the thinking process. Using all the modes of thinking in balance requires that we understand each mode, what it can do for us, and what we can do with it.

The three modes are:

1. *Rational thinking.* This is thinking from the observed facts in front of us, using reason and logic to reach a conclusion. It is thinking using information from direct observation and gathered from reliable sources, open and available to anyone who wishes to look. It is commonly called "scientific thinking" and has to do with here-and-now, immediately experienced reality. Fact-based rational thinking tells us, "This is so because an effect has been observed and can be reproduced whenever desired."

This mode is considered the most reliable and valid. It is open to distortions of perception and interpretation, but the possibility of reobservation and measurement provides its control on error.

2. *Intuitive thinking.* This is thinking that occurs without the conscious use of reason or logic. An idea simply wells up from the unconscious mind in response to the perception of a problem or issue. Information for this kind of thinking comes from the integration of stored fragments, facts, and impressions that have accumulated over the years. It is the distillation of experience and is variously called "wisdom," "feel," or "conviction." It may be based on fact or fable in unknown proportion, but it is at the same time the most relevant summary of all that has been acquired with respect to a given subject by a capable observer. As such, it is the concentrated essence of what a person has seen and experienced over the years. Its errors are those of assumption and imprecise memory. Once intuitive knowledge has been verified and proven rationally, it is just as reliable and valid as any other data.

3. *Creative or imaginative thinking.* This is thinking that reaches out beyond what is now into what could be. It puts known elements together to form new ideas and visions. It is future-oriented, rather than focused on the present time. It draws on observation, experience, knowledge, and the indefinable ability that each person has to arrange common elements into new patterns. "Invention," "insight," and "inspiration" are common words that describe this phenomenon. Its errors derive from its unwillingness to acknowledge the restraints of reality. Once a vision has been stated as a concrete proposal, however, it is open to rational test just as any other statement might be. Once tested and proven, it becomes solid data to be used rationally.

Collaboration and the Modes of Thinking

When people collaborate to address a problem, they use all three modes of thinking. The first contributions are usually *rational,* the facts as known. These are related to one another through logic to form a story of the situation, which is invariably incomplete and missing information.

To make up for the lack of facts, *intuitive* ideas, derived from experience and drawn out of memory, are contributed as the problem triggers a person to respond with something that appears relevant; this idea in turn acts as a trigger to someone else, producing a second response, which leads to a third. Intuitive thinking produces a wealth of ideas, one built on another. These ideas are unsorted, incompletely stated, and inelegant in the beginning, representing bits and pieces taken from the pasts of the contributors. They become more complete and respectable as they are discussed and traded back and forth.

When ideas from intuitive thinking have been stated, they are subjected to rational thinking to determine how solid and reliable they are: Is this true? Can it be confirmed by observation and experiment? Does it make logical good sense? What conclusions can we draw from this? Rational thinking seeks to sort out fact from speculation. Ideas that can be proven and that check out against accepted knowledge are treated as solid rational data, while those that fail to meet the test are discarded.

As the body of information and ideas grows, *creative* or *imaginative* thinking comes into play: Could this have been a possible factor? Suppose we changed it this way. . . . Far-out ideas are entertained, evaluated rationally, and either accepted or rejected. Everything that seems relevant is considered, but only those ideas that meet the test of logic are added to the common understanding.

Open discussion is the method of collaboration. This thinking out loud is not aimless, since it is focused on a mutually understood subject and task. Its discipline is relevance. Ideas come out, are examined, and are put together to form new ideas. Open discussion demands a safe arena in which ideas can be put forward. This is often a face-to-face meeting, but it doesn't have to be; ideas can be contributed and examined over the phone, by fax or e-mail, on the screen of a computer, or by any other medium that allows for interchange of information. The requirement of a safe arena allows ideas to be seen and examined by others without censure, ridicule, or premature rejection.

Examination doesn't take place instantly. People who are collaborating need time to think and chew over ideas, some more than others. The safe arena needs some mechanism for holding ideas while the people involved have a chance to digest and understand them. A blackboard, piece of paper, or easel pad can do the job of holding information and making it visually available to everyone, and software that allows ideas to be collected and displayed on a computer screen is excellent for this purpose. But verbal response, simply saying something relevant, is not enough. Ideas are transitory and must be saved until they can be appreciated, particulary those that come from experience and may be poorly expressed at first. Collaboration is thinking together about the same thing at the same time, which implies having the information there to see and understand in common. If it is only spoken, a good idea may die as soon as the echoes fade and another statement takes its place.

And so goes collaboration. Ideas from all modes of thinking are discussed, evaluated, and either accepted or rejected. The fund of new ideas grows, and new combinations of ideas appear. By drawing upon the rational, intuitive, and creative modes of thought of your best-informed co-workers, you can sharpen the resolution and enhance its complexity until it reaches dimensions that go beyond what any of the participants might have achieved alone, as participants' experience, creativity, or rational thought supplied what others' funds of knowledge lacked.

The Ability to Think

Managerial thinking ability is an underused resource. Only a fraction of the available mental horsepower is put to work by most managers. Too much of what they do is by habit, doing what others have done before them. All of us have seen decisions that never should have been made and plans put into effect that overlooked or ignored vital information. Why? Part of the explanation lies in outmoded tradition, and part in the fact that many managers don't understand how to apply their thinking skills on the job. Both of these hindrances can be easily overcome.

Our traditions glorify the fact-based, hard-nosed rational-thinking approach. "Scientific thinking" put us on the moon and gets the credit for our technological advances. Part true, part mythology. Intuition, plus experience and learning, plus imagination, all play an essential part. Scientists have inspirations, gut feelings. They put together what they know from formal sources and experience, combine it with common sense, and imagine what it all means. Then they go into the laboratory with a specific hypothesis, and in due time proof emerges, positive or negative.

Richard Feynman, of the *Challenger* presidential commission, is an example of the joining of the intuitive and the factual. His gut, experience, and common sense told him that cold temperatures were involved in the loss of the *Challenger*. He then put some O-ring material into his glass of ice water to test his hypothesis, to *confirm* what he thought, and there was the proof. Wide-spectrum, all-modes thinking solves problems. This same combination of techniques was used in the work that won him the 1965 Nobel prize in physics.

We "use our heads" every day and call it common sense. We get an idea, an inspiration, a hunch, or a feeling. We then subject that idea or hunch to logic to see whether it will stand up to reason. If it makes sense and can be tested and turns out to be sound, we go ahead with it. If it falls apart, we try again. Common sense and scientific thinking are much alike. Logical, rational thinking is *orderly* common sense, if you will. We should be aware of how valid and important common sense is, moving from idea or intuition to a logical proposition that can be tested, and should use it without apology every chance we get.

So glorified has the rational "scientific" approach become that we hesitate to draw on our experience and informed hunches in public. We have come to think of intuition as something inferior and marginal, and we are reluctant to let others know we have thoughts like that. So we remain silent and let a great idea die because the traditions of management don't support intuition and creative thinking. We cheat ourselves when we let that happen, because there is plenty of room for common sense in management.

It's easy to change that tradition. You have only to ask your co-workers, "Can you think of anything from your experience that would explain this?" to create new rules of inquiry. By your question, you have given your colleagues permission to think in a broader way. Asking "How do you feel about this?" will open their thinking even more. Asking "Can you imagine . . . " will open it up still more. When people understand that it is legitimate to draw on other modes of thinking, they will respond; when you indicate that you are interested in their intuition about something, they will tell you what they think. By the questions you ask, you set the boundaries of the discussion; whether you and your co-workers use all three modes of thinking is really up to you.

Many managers have learned rigid ways of thinking from a management environment that has been hostile to intuition and creativity and that has discouraged the participation of colleagues in management decisions. They have learned to think and act in the style of their predecessors and their teachers. So they carry forward what they believe is proper management behavior and do what has worked in the past, with little motivation to experiment or acquire new ways of thinking.

Telling your colleagues to think more broadly will have no effect. You have to show them how it works by example. Once they see that making use of rational, intuitive, and creative modes of thought is easy and effective, they will feel free to try. In their private lives they have used all these modes since infancy, so they don't have to learn something new. All they have to learn is that it is all right to use these same ways of thinking in the management world.

To encourage people to think a different way, you focus their attention on an aspect of a problem and a mode of thinking by asking them for specific information. Suppose that a gasket has failed on a high-pressure pump. You get rational, factual information by asking, "What happened here?" People will then tell you what they saw. You get intuitive knowledge about the failure of gaskets by asking, "In your experience, what would cause a gasket like that to blow?" People will then recall past examples of failure and tell you things you hadn't even heard of. You get their creative ideas by asking, "How do you think we can install this gasket so that it won't blow again?" You will hear ideas about gaskets that you never thought of before.

When you ask a question, you set the boundaries of relevance and the mode of thinking to be used. Everyone will be thinking about the same thing in the same way at the same time; collaboration will occur, and ideas will build that will generate new ideas. Create a safe arena within which your people can suggest ideas, lead them to use all their thinking abilities, and you will achieve better resolutions.

Chapters 6 through 15 talk about the tasks that will let you manage beyond the ordinary and suggest ways how each can be done. But it will be up to you to select the ways that fit your situation and your style. Think about what you need to do and the best way for you to do it with this problem and these people, at this time and in this setting. Think about the tasks to be completed and how you will get the collaboration you need from your people. You will find yourself getting more done, with less strain and effort and at a higher level of quality—and liking it. You can define and promote management thinking in the way that will help you the most, embracing all three modes of thinking and the practice of collaboration.

Note

1. William P. Rogers, chairman, *Report to the President by the Presidential Commission on the Space Shuttle Challenger Accident* (Washington, D.C.: U.S. Government Printing Office, 1986).

3

A Checklist for Managing Beyond the Ordinary

About now you're probably thinking, "Ten tasks! Three modes of thinking! How can I remember this when I'm already over-burdened and overstressed and have twice as much to do as I have time for?"

Managers can't create more time in the day. Yet when they look ahead, they see the pressures on them increasing. They have to find ways to do what needs to be done in less time and with better results. They need a friend to help carry the load.

But managers aren't the only people who must deal with details under pressure and conditions of complexity. We need to look at how others handle the same kind of problems to see if there is something we can learn from them. Have others found a way of working that makes it easier to meet all the demands on them?

You're at the airport, waiting to board your plane. You see the first officer walking around on the tarmac, checking the wheels, looking at the flaps, inspecting the engines. It's the five hundredth time he's done this, yet he carefully goes through the routine. He doesn't question the checklist of items to be inspected or decide that this time it isn't necessary to complete it. He follows the routine, step by step. His checklist helps him focus his attention and remember everything he needs to and protects him from making mistakes. At the same time, up in the cockpit, the captain is going through an even more detailed checklist, which he follows religiously. That's why the statistics show that it's ten times safer to ride a plane than to drive your own car.

We have put together a checklist procedure for managing beyond the ordinary that sets out the tasks to be completed and the questions you might ask to get your resource people to collaborate with you. You can decide how closely you should follow the checklist in any given situation. We recommend that you use it every time you have a problem; it will remind you where you are and what you should do as you and your colleagues work your way through to a resolution.

The increasing complexity of today's business environment and the stiff penalties for making a wrong decision have made a checklist procedure for management thinking essential. When information comes at you from all sides, by e-mail, fax, conference call, print-outs, conversations out in the hall, memos that pile up on the desk, and team computing, you need all the help you can get to keep on top of your job. The Wright brothers didn't need a checklist when airplanes were made of wood, canvas, and wire. But the airline pilot does now, and so does the manager. You can't afford to forget or overlook something important. Failure costs too much.

The Checklist Procedure

The process of problem resolution involves ten tasks that must be carried out to make the analysis complete. They are the necessary steps in the process of thinking through any issue or problem. The procedure says what the thinking product needs to be, what must be accomplished each step of the way. It also serves as a road map, telling you the route you must travel from here to there. If you are working with a group of resource people and they are following the same map, you will all be thinking about the same thing at the same time, and collaboration will be easy.

Each of the ten tasks is clearly defined and concrete, and each makes sense and is easy to visualize and focus on. Task 5 says that you must know and be able to prove the cause of the problem before you can resolve it most efficiently; how you find the cause and confirm it—by rational, intuitive, or creative means, or any combination of the three—is up to the collaborating group. This makes common sense to those who are trying to resolve the problem and allows everyone to contribute some information about the cause. The goal of the collaboration is defined, but people are left completely free to decide how they will use what they know together in order to reach their objective.

The procedure is a list of requirements to be met, with comments concerning techniques that may be helpful. Chapters 6 through 15 also offer how-to-do-it suggestions. It is intended to help you make sure that nothing has been overlooked, skipped, or forgotten if you are to manage beyond the ordinary.

Task 1: Understanding the Problem Situation

The task here is for the group working on the problem to get information about the problem, sort it out, set priorities, and achieve a shared understanding of what is going on—in short, to build a solid base of information from which to conduct an analysis and produce agreement on the situation to be resolved.

Most attempts at problem resolution start with an incomplete understanding of the problem situation. It is assumed that everyone sees the problem the same way, but this is seldom the case. Instead, people have to gather more information and correct misunderstandings as they go along. Getting it right the first time, getting a straight story to work from, makes collaboration possible.

Task 2: Understanding the Purpose to Be Served

The objective of this task is to review the purpose to be served. The group seeks an answer to the question "What are we trying to do here? Is this what we *should* be doing?" It asks whether the purpose is appropriate or whether it is out of date or inadequate in some way and creates a clearer, more useful statement of objectives, giving everyone a common understanding of what the group hopes to accomplish.

Failure to ask this question often results in fixing up something that should be rejected or changed. And holding onto an obsolete or inadequate goal blocks progress. Coming to an agreement on what is to be accomplished often opens new pathways of action that are more effective than those that were previously accepted.

Task 3: Involving the People Who Can Help Resolve the Problem

The purpose of this task is to determine what kind of information the group will need to resolve the problem and who has it and to decide who can best contribute the needed information and knowledge. It is also to determine how to get the ideas the group needs from those who have them and how to obtain their commitment to think together to develop a resolution everyone can support.

Many attempts to resolve a problem involve too many or the wrong people. Thinking through who has the best information, who can work together, and who will need to implement the resolution when it is completed saves time and eliminates many of the endless meetings that managers hate. Getting the resource people's commitment to work toward a common goal directs everyone's attention in the same direction.

Task 4: Getting a Complete and Accurate Picture of the Problem

The task here is to get accurate information about what is wrong and what in the situation is deficient and should be repaired, improved, corrected, or avoided. It is also to identify what is unique about the problem and what changes may have contributed to its cause. Finally, it is to organize the information visually so that everyone can understand it in the same way.

Attempts to resolve problems often fail to describe the problems in detail and use terms so general that they can be understood by different people in different ways, so issues often get lost or overlooked. When people don't share a common perception of a problem, they cannot agree on what is causing it or what should be done about it. Achieving an accurate portrait of the problem that everyone can see and understand is a necessary step toward collaboration aimed at developing the problem's resolution.

Task 5: Finding the Cause and Proving It

The goal of this task is to determine beyond doubt what caused the problem, using the knowledge of change to find it and proving the cause by logic and experiment.

Too often, people think they how what has caused a problem, but they aren't sure or have several possible causes and don't know which one is the real cause. They take a number of actions and hope that one of them will solve the problem, but they can't be certain the problem has really been resolved and must wait to see if it goes away. When people can prove the cause of a problem and know that they understand the problem, they can collaborate on finding the best way to handle it.

Task 6: Setting the Criteria for Effective Action

The purpose of this task is to determine what needs to be repaired, improved, corrected, or avoided to achieve a complete resolution of the problem, to define the criteria or requirements of an ideal resolution, and to assign weights of importance if necessary.

People often accept the minimum action that will handle a problem and never ask what an ideal resolution would be, thereby losing their opportunity to improve the situation. Setting out the criteria of an ideal resolution gives them an understanding of what can be done and opens up possibilities that otherwise would never be recognized.

Task 7: Finding the Best Actions to Resolve the Problem

The purpose of this task is to draw on the experience, knowledge, and judgment of the best-informed people to form a pool of best actions through which to resolve the problem and then to select the most cost-effective of these to form a first attempt at a resolution.

People often opt for the first solution to a problem that occurs to them, which is usually complex, expensive, incomplete, and difficult to implement. Searching for other actions invariably produces simpler alternatives that can be combined to form a better way to resolve the problem. Working with a pool of best actions challenges creativity and produces superior results.

Task 8: Creating a Workable First-Draft Plan of Action

In this task, the group organizes the selected actions into a feasible time sequence for implementation, checking interactions between actions and balancing short- and long-term considerations to form a workable first-draft plan. It also searches out potential weaknesses that might materialize during implementation. Finally, it seeks a common understanding and agreement as to what actions should be taken. Creating a workable first draft helps to identify and eliminate future problems and greatly reduces the number of unpleasant surprises that will arise later on.

Task 9: Fine-Tuning the Plan into a Program of Action

The purpose of this task is to fine-tune the plan to fit with the purposes and practices of the organization, consolidate and simplify actions, and strengthen any areas of weakness. It also assigns accountability, conducts a risk analysis of its effects on other plans and activities, and achieves agreement as to the actions to be recommended.

Efforts to consolidate and simplify actions and to strengthen weak areas are often overlooked. A thorough risk analysis is not usually part of the planning procedure; instead, potential problems are usually left to be dealt with only if the need arises. But all of these actions are essential if the plan is to be implemented smoothly and to resolve the problem effectively.

Task 10: Communicating to Gain Understanding and Acceptance

The final task is to identify the audience and other significant targets for communication and to determine what their objectives, needs, and expectations are so that recommendations for action can be presented in terms consistent with those needs. At this point the group presents the complete logic of the resolution so that those who will approve the resolution and put it into effect can understand and accept it. This task also includes adding the decision and its logic to the institutional memory of the organization so that others may understand it in the future.

You can use this checklist procedure as a guide to make sure you are doing what you need to do. It is not an iron-bound, dictatorial format that robs you of judgment and the ability to adapt. To use it, mentally check each task in turn. On the first task, ask yourself, "Do I fully understand this problem situation?" If you can truthfully answer yes, go on to the next. If there is a doubt in your mind, get more information about the situation to make sure. Always take the fail-safe way and assume that there might be something you don't know. When you are satisfied that you know all you need to know, go to the next task.

About 15 percent of the managers who read this will say, "I hope my colleagues use these ideas. They need them, but I don't. I do all these things already." There is little hope for this segment of the population. People who know everything already can't learn and won't change. The rest will put these procedures in their managerial tool boxes and use them where they think they apply.

Levels of Involvement in Problem Resolution

A procedure has to be used by someone to do any good. But who will actually make use of it? It is intended for you as a manager, but not you alone. It is for all the people who will be involved in resolving the problem, and it can be used by anyone, on any aspect of any problem. Your co-workers will use whatever parts of it are relevant to their involvement, depending on their part in the problem resolution and what they need to do.

There are three levels of involvement in the resolution of any problem. At the first level, there is the person on the spot, the one who is administratively responsible for achieving a resolution. We call this person the *mover* because he or she makes the whole project go. The mover may be the person who discovers the problem, the person to whom it is assigned by someone else, the person who inherits it, or the poor soul who is unlucky enough to be standing there when it happens. The mover decides the procedure to be followed and leads the rest of the people through the ten tasks to resolve it. The mover may be an executive, a manager, a supervisor, or anyone else.

The mover enlists the aid of a few people who have some knowledge and functional responsibility for the problem and a stake in the outcome. These form the *working group,* the second level of involvement. This level includes two or three people who know a good deal about the situation and who will help the mover organize the project, pull in the information, and draw whatever conclusions are warranted. For a small problem, the mover may not need a working group but can perform these functions alone. For a more complex problem, the mover may assemble a nucleus of four or five co-workers to help. The size of the working group should always remain as small as possible.

At the third level are the *resource people* who have the knowledge, experience, and opinions needed to resolve the problem. These people are drawn in by the mover and the working group as required. They are not permanent fixtures; they are involved only when they have something relevant to contribute. Someone may have information about one aspect of the problem but know nothing of the other issues; that person is brought into the process only when that particular aspect is considered. When each person in the group knows what tasks are to be completed and is following the same procedure, there is little wasted time or effort.

This process is in contrast to the more common procedure in which all the people who might possibly have an interest in the matter, and a lot who have none whatsoever, are herded together. They often find themselves asking, "What am I doing here?" and never get an adequate answer. Involvement should be selective, based on the merits of the individual contributor. That way, involvement becomes a precision tool in the hands of the manager that allows her to go beyond the ordinary. Nor does everyone have to be physically present. You want the relevent information, not necessarily the physical presence of those who have the information. A resource person can contribute by phone or fax or through a computer just as well as if he were sitting there.

GENERATING RESULTS THROUGH COLLABORATION

Because one mill owned by a paper company is in an isolated part of western Canada, it generates its own electrical power from steam. One time, as the mill was getting ready for a visit of the company's executive vice president and board of directors the next day, the generator went down in midmorning. A backup unit was put on line, but most of the mill's activities were shut down because the power available was inadequate to support full operations. The mill manager told his head of production to find a resolution, quick.

The head of production, the *mover,* carried out a quick inspection, which showed the generator to be damaged beyond repair. It was old and had been scheduled for replacement the following year. Now a new one would have to be found and installed in a hurry. The mover called in the head of power generation and the plant engineer to form a three-person working group. They talked with supervisors from production and from the power house and listed the characteristics of an ideal generation system. It had to produce a certain level of power at peak times, be compatible with the present electrical system, be immediately available, be operable by the existing personnel, and much more. Three potentially acceptable generation systems were identified.

They then sought specific information about each system from their resource people. Some of these were people within the plant or at other plants who shared what they knew; some were representatives from the three companies making the alternative systems; some were outside experts who provided data on performance, reliability, cost of operation, and other matters. Most of these contacts were by phone, fax, or e-mail. The working group pulled the information together and evaluated it, with suggestions from their in-plant colleagues. By late afternoon the mover was able to go to the mill manager with a documented, well-reasoned recommendation as to the best system.

The executive VP and members of the board arrived the next

morning to find the mill on standby. A meeting was called, and the mover presented the problem and the mill's recommendation for the replacement system. A discussion followed, and the members of the working group were able to answer all the questions raised by the EVP and the board members. A decision was made on the spot, and the new system was ordered before noon, just twenty-four hours after the old system failed. It should be noted that the new system was not simply a replacement but a different generating system that would bring greater efficiency to the plant. The group had resolved the problem and improved the system at the same time.

The people at the mill had a shared understanding of what tasks needed completion to ensure the best resolution of the problem. They had a common procedure and were able to reason together to arrive at a recommendation they could all support. Many people were involved, yet at no time was there a face-to-face meeting of more than six. They recruited the best knowledge and the best information available but avoided having all the bodies together in one place for hours of debate.

When you and your colleagues follow this procedure, you can all think and work together, talking about the same things at the same time. All your thinking will be in tune. You can delegate responsibility to other people because you will know that they are going to go about the job the same way you would. A common procedure and checklist will remind everyone what questions to ask and what information to gather. And you can evaluate your work against the procedure to make sure that all the tasks have been completed.

You can't create more time in your managerial day, but you can be more efficient in using the time and the resources available. One way to do this is to understand the tasks that enable you to manage beyond the ordinary and gather them in a procedure that will guide how you and your co-workers spend time and effort. When you all follow the same way of thinking, the barriers of confusion, distance, and location will vanish.

How to Do It

Chapters 6 through 15 explain the how-to-do-its for each of the ten tasks. They set out what to do in order to satisfy the requirements for complete problem resolution. They also give examples of managers who have put these ideas to work to achieve resolutions that have gone beyond the ordinary. Chapters 16 through 18 tell you how to motivate your people and install the system.

If you follow these guidelines and apply your own techniques of managing, you will be able to carry out the complete resolution of a problem from start to finish. You will leave nothing undone and overlook nothing. You will do the best possible job of resolving whatever problem you undertake, given the information and resources you have to work with.

If you don't use it, you won't gain benefit from it. The captain of your airplane has to follow a checklist to ensure that you get to your destination in one piece. If you want to manage beyond the ordinary, you need to internalize the ten steps in this procedure and use them every time you confront a management problem. And you need to have your colleagues use the procedure along with you. If you all follow it, you will all move in the same direction, in an orderly manner, and as productively as possible.

4

Barriers to Managing Beyond the Ordinary

If managing beyond the ordinary makes so much sense, why don't all managers do it? Because there are barriers to managing beyond the ordinary. People usually hesitate to try something different because they're afraid they may have to pay for it later. These fears need to be faced before they feel free to take on a new way of doing anything.

The Five Barriers

The Barrier of Tradition

The first barrier is *tradition,* or habit, especially in our conception of the role of the manager. Our early ideas about management came from the military. There was the leader, waving his sword and directing his troops, and there were the soldiers, marching in front of him, doing what they were told. The officers had the ideas and the soldiers carried them out or died in the attempt.

Not so long ago, it was considered disrespectful for a soldier or sailor to suggest to an officer a better way of doing something, and the soldier or sailor could be flogged for his efforts. And it wasn't that long ago that a worker on the assembly line made a suggestion for improvement to Henry Ford and was told, "You aren't paid to think; you're paid to do what you're told. We have people in the office to do the thinking for you."

It's hard to get over that tradition of top-down, inspired wisdom from above, because for centuries it worked well enough. The superior had the ideas and gave the orders, and the inferior carried them out. The superior told, and the inferior did. The superior knew he was superior because he had a title that said so. General Custer was superior; he wouldn't listen to his trackers and scouts who said there were a lot of angry Indians up ahead, and he paid the price for ignoring the people around him who knew more than he did.

The barrier of tradition is real. We are quick to say, "We're not like that!" But there is a shadow of the top-down, command-and-control philosophy in all of us, and more than a shadow in some, in spite of the fact that we've been lectured about teamwork since the 1970s. Most of us learned to manage in an organization that was top-down and that operated in a simpler environment than we face today. It is hard for us to realize that things are different now and to call for different approaches, to understand that the rank-and-file worker is a specialist who may know things that the executive in the corporate tower hasn't even heard of.

In order to get the best out of what we know, we need all-ways management: top-down, bottom-up, and in-and-out-from-all-sides. Wherever the ideas are, we need to bring them together to create better ways of doing things. The habit of thinking that wisdom can be found only at the top is one barrier that keeps this coming together from happening. We need to change our definition of the role of the manager from one who gives orders to one who asks questions to bring knowledge and ideas together to resolve problems.

The Barrier of Reverence for Individualism and Competition

Our intense reverence for *individualism and competition* is perhaps the greatest barrier to managing beyond the ordinary. Nearly everything we do is focused on the individual, and almost all the encouragement we receive is for individual effort. We are graded on what we accomplish, receive promotions for what we do as individuals, are praised for good work in school, and are urged to do better throughout every stage of our lives, measuring our success against the performance of others. We are paid and rewarded for what we do as individuals. It is little wonder that we think so much about our individual output and what we believe we can and should get.

We need to be honest about this. We are born individuals and will die individuals. Socialization comes later for all of us. Few of us immediately think of seeking the advice of others when a problem or need for decision comes up. We try to do it all ourselves. It is natural for us to think individual first, group, team, or community second. Doing it ourselves seems the best way to control the outcome. And trying to run faster than the other guy is also natural. What is not helpful is letting individualism and competition get in the way of working with others for the good of all.

Humans survived only by pooling their best ideas and efforts for their own salvation. They worked together to find food and shelter because that was the only way they could do it. They found that a person could be an individual in competition with others and still collaborate on problems of survival. That is a lesson we need to learn again. We need a warning that goes off in our heads, saying, "This is getting complicated—find out more about it and get someone else's point of view before taking action." We think it would be better to hear that warning too early than too late.

We carry the tendency to act as individuals over into the world of business. But one individual cannot produce a circuit board or a sales campaign that works or anything else of importance in this complex, interactive setting. Virtually everything that counts is achieved by the efforts of people working together. People have to share what they know in order to deal with the world around them. Thinking and working together gives people greater control over what happens than they would have working alone.

You can think and work in cooperation with other individuals without losing your autonomy as a person. Individualism and collaboration do not constitute an either-or choice. You do not have to give up your individuality to collaborate with others. People collaborating to find a better way of doing something are just a group of individuals who are working together to achieve a purpose that will benefit them all.

We need to find a balance between individualism and competition—not enough individualism to keep us from working with others, yet enough to keep us from becoming lost in the crowd. We need to be individuals in our willingness to take responsibility and to accept blame if we make a mistake. We need a balance between individual drive and the desire to work with others. We need to be competitive enough to take risks, get out in front to lead, and want to do better, even as we collaborate with others to achieve results that we cannot hope to produce by ourselves.

The Barrier of the Effort Involved

The third barrier to managing beyond the ordinary is the thought, effort, and discipline that such management requires. Going beyond doesn't occur automatically. People have to think about the problem and what to do next, and then act to make it happen. This means being constantly alert for things that aren't good enough and that offer opportunities for improvement. It's hard work to think; to think all the time is even harder. It's easier to just rock along and do things by habit, in the same old way as before. It's easier to do only what clamors to be done. After all, "If it ain't broke, don't fix it."

Doing things by habit, not by thinking, would be all right as long as nothing changed and nothing new arose as a challenge. But in business, things are always changing, so you have to ask questions and know what is going on. You have to be looking for what's new and different in the world around you. Adapting to change is one of the key tasks of the manager. Drifting along is suicidal and self-destructive.

Looking at every problem as a new situation calls for a redirection of effort rather than for more effort. Instead of adding to your management load, you need to do the management job in a different way. Then you will be substituting a better way for an inadequate one.

The Barrier of Complacency

Complacency is the fourth barrier to managing beyond the ordinary. "We're doing all right," some people say, when it is obvious they could be doing better. "We're not the leaders in our field, but we're not at the tail end, either." Yet. Denial does not win any prizes in management. Continue to be complacent, and pretty soon all you will see is the dust generated by your competitors as they leave you behind.

You have to do better each day because each day your competitors are trying their best to be better than you. Nothing stands still; things either go forward or go backward. Denying the need for improvement can be fatal because it lulls you into not trying, and that automatically gives the edge to the other guy. What you need is a resolve to improve your handling of problems each time you face a new one.

The Barrier of Insecurity and Fear

The fifth barrier is *insecurity and fear*, the idea that if we turn away from what has been moderately successful in the past, we're taking a chance on failure! We'll try something new and make fools of ourselves because it might not work! People will see us bumbling around, and they'll think we don't know what we're doing! If we ask questions, people will think we're uninformed! We'll lose our reputations. Or it will take too much time. Managers are afraid that change will be additive, that one task will pile on top of another; they don't consider seeking a new way of managing to take the place of the old and perhaps saving time in the process. It is easier to say, "No, never" than it is to assess the prospect of change and what it might gain.

We're afraid that if we let others participate, someone will screw up, things will get out of control, and we'll get blamed. If we let others take over, who knows what will happen then? Better keep control and stick with what we know, even if it isn't perfect. At least we'll know what's going on.

The trouble is that fear is disabling. It freezes people into immobility and keeps them from progressing. It keeps managers doing the same old thing when they could be moving ahead. We don't want to take foolish chances, but we don't want to turn into pillars of stone, either.

Eliminating the Barriers

The barriers we have described are real. They keep people from growing unless the people can find ways to get around them. Many managers find they can get past these barriers, but many more come to a stop before them and give up. Let's look at these barriers and see how they can be reduced or overcome.

Overcoming Tradition

Tradition, or habit, is the first barrier: "I've done it this way for years, and I can't be expected to change now." Some say this is natural, that we humans are resistant to change. Not so. Humans are the most changeable animals known. We will change the way we do things in an instant if we think it will do us some good. Remember how quickly we accepted cellular phones? People are not resistant to change. They resist only changes that threaten to hurt them or for which the benefits are uncertain.

If you want to change tradition and habit, first lay the benefits out clearly. Convince your colleagues that good things will come from the change. Show them how life will be easier, fuller, safer, and happier if they adopt the new way of doing things and how the old way can be replaced safely as the new way proves itself. We give tradition its power, because we create our beliefs ourselves; we can take that power away and change our habits as soon as an old belief is replaced by a new one. Convince yourself and others that managing beyond the ordinary will be good for everyone, more interesting, personally satisfying, and maybe even fun. Then the barrier of tradition will vanish.

PUTTING PEOPLE AT EASE

Arnold Johnson had been a tough, top-down manager for years. A colonel in the army, he had retired and joined a major electronics company, where he had risen rapidly. As Johnson began to mellow with age and thought over his role as manager, he convinced himself he should change. But the people under him were all top-down, since they had learned management from him. How could he change their habits? Maybe if he tried another way, on the quiet, and showed them how good it was, they'd follow him.

So Johnson asked a subordinate for her opinion on how a difficult problem might be handled. After the subordinate got over her shock at being asked her opinion, she was pleased to share her expertise with the boss. It worked so well that Johnson asked another, and another, then another. In a few weeks, all the people under him were sharing what they knew and thought and liking it. They were interacting in a totally new way. They had changed their habits and didn't even realize it. They saw Johnson's asking questions not as a sign of ignorance but as an overdue recognition of how good they were and how much they knew. All they were aware of was that things were going better than they ever had before.

Overcoming Reverence for Individualism and Competition

The second barrier is our dedication to *individualism and competition*. This barrier—the fear of losing one's individual place in the organization—is demolished through a simple demonstration that one can contribute without in any way risking the loss of one's identity.

If you ask another person his ideas about something, he will probably be flattered and happy to give them. You, an individual, have approached another person, another sovereign individual, and shared ideas. You haven't reduced your standing or the other person's but have reinforced that person's perception of himself as an individual who has ideas that are worth listening to, and that is a sincere compliment.

The belief in individual effort cannot be disarmed by argument because most of the assumptions made about individualism are emotional, not logical. The reliance on individual effort and constant competition is a near-religious belief to many. To counter people's fear of losing their individuality, it is necessary to demonstrate that working together in a noncompetitive way and being an individual are compatible. Once people find that they lose nothing through cooperation and gain a great deal, the barrier will disappear.

A RESIDENT GENIUS

One electronics company had an extremely creative scientist as one of its key people. David Kroeger was a very bright man, considered a genius by those around him. He modestly agreed that he was indeed a genius and held nearly a hundred patents as proof of it. Kroeger felt that most of his colleagues were beneath him and that they made stupid decisions about how to run the organization. Kroeger also felt that his time was too valuable to waste in meetings where policy decisions were debated. He considered himself a unique individual and had a horror of being caught up in "groupthink" sessions at which the decisions made represented the lowest intellectual denominator of the members assembled.

The CEO, Wes Logan, caught Kroeger in the hallway and asked for his ideas on an issue. He got a worthwhile opinion, which he relayed to the policy-making group. He reported back to Kroeger how his inputs had been utilized in the decision process. This pleased Kroeger, and he offered to share his wisdom again in the future. When a complex problem came up a short time later, Logan asked Kroeger if he would present his views to the management group in person, as an outside consultant. He did and enjoyed a spirited discussion with its members about the matter at hand, contributing a number of valuable ideas. And the others accepted his ideas without feeling overwhelmed by his genius.

When Kroeger realized that he could contribute his ideas without losing his position as resident genius, he became an important resource for the company, taking part in the decision-making process when he had knowledge and experience that were relevant. He later confided to a colleague that he'd found his co-workers smarter than he'd expected. Kroeger couldn't have been convinced by argument, but Logan had shown him that he could collaborate with others and still remain a unique individual, and even enjoy it.

Overcoming the Effort Involved

The third barrier is the *thought, effort, and discipline* that is required to manage beyond the ordinary. Superior management requires a person to develop a program of information-handling techniques, as well as to think about the problem itself. Managing the process of going beyond the ordinary is sometimes seen as more difficult than dealing with the problem itself.

To deal with this barrier, it is necessary to create a procedure that manages the details of the process. Like a program in a computer, this procedure describes what needs to be done next, provides a structure within which to consider the problem and organize the information, and offers a standard by which to determine one's progress. It lets the manager think about the problem while the procedure takes care of the details.

You have already seen such a procedure—the ten tasks. The chapters to come show how to use it. If you follow the procedure, you will arrive at the best resolution possible.

Overcoming Complacency

The fourth barrier is *complacency,* the hypnotic assumption that everything is just fine and that there's no need to worry.

The only way to remove this barrier is to shatter it with the truth through management shock therapy. How do you stand, compared with your competitors? What problems keep you from achieving all your goals? What do your customers complain about? Is everybody happy? If not, why not?

Get out the facts. Hold up the mirror, and be sure everyone can see what is reflected in it. Make yourself and others uncomfortable enough to want to improve things. If the need for change isn't burned into everyone's mind, nothing will ever get any better.

Some say management change won't occur until the corporate culture changes. That's wrong. The corporate culture changes because management perception and behavior have changed, not the other way around. You can't change the corporate culture by writing another memo. When people see they have problems and work together to resolve them, the culture will change to encourage collaboration. It all starts with waking people out of their complacency and forcing them to see that they have serious problems that need attention.

Helen Porter, a manager in a large and very self-satisfied chemical company, wanted to introduce a better way of resolving problems. But her colleagues weren't interested. They didn't think there was anything wrong with the way they were presently handling them. So Porter dug a skeleton out of the closet, an extremely expensive problem that had been mismanaged a few years before. She researched the situation and documented her findings. Then she presented the case at a meeting.

Porter was dramatic in her telling, and she made the mistakes and false solutions seem ridiculous, which wasn't hard. She had everybody laughing. After telling about one particularly stupid attempt to solve the problem, she asked, "Can you believe this?" The group couldn't and agreed that any company like that ought to go under. Then she told her listeners that it was their own company and described when this had happened, what divisions and people had been involved, and the huge costs and consequences. It got very quiet in the room, particularly when she showed that a better way of approaching problems would have uncovered the cause and put the entire matter to rest within a few days, instead of the year-plus that it actually took. Porter had their attention now, along with their willingness to entertain new ideas. Complacency as a barrier to doing something different had disappeared.

Overcoming Insecurity and Fear

The fifth barrier is *insecurity and fear*. This is a real problem, for organizations don't have much sympathy for managers who goof up on important matters. What can you do about this? Don't goof up. Make your efforts to manage beyond the ordinary secure and fail-safe. The worst thing you can do, when trying a new technique, is to make a big deal of it. If you yell, "Look at me! I'm about to do something wonderful!" you raise all kinds of expectations and set yourself up for embarrassment and failure. Instead, take your time and start out slow and easy. Pick a problem that you have to deal with anyway, and then apply the procedures you are learning about. Involve other people without rocking the boat. Then assess how you have done and how you might do better next time.

Try it again, quietly. Develop your skills and confidence. Experiment and explore. Allow yourself to grow into managing beyond the ordinary. Each time you try it, you will be better at it, and you will convince others by example. Before long, you will have a movement under way, without ever publicly challenging the old techniques you are displacing.

Introducing a new idea quietly is fail-safe because you never stake your reputation on a single, dramatic outcome, announced loudly in advance. You change the practice of management by evolution, rather than by revolution. After it is all over, when you are satisfied with the results, you can point out what you have done. But you can play it safe while you are learning by keeping a low profile.

Involving others is fail-safe; their input will confirm that you were right in the first place, or prove that you were wrong, giving you a chance to alter your position, or enable you to learn something new that you otherwise wouldn't have known. Your colleagues will help you, not take over. They will give you their ideas and recommendations, and you will decide whether to accept them. This approach is fail-safe because you involve the people who know the most about the problem and exclude those who don't know or can't contribute. You retain control over your project without encroaching on the creativity or satisfaction of the people you involve. Asking questions and sharing ideas is a lot more friendly than giving orders.

Managing beyond the ordinary is fail-safe because it provides you with ways to prove and test your conclusions as you go along. You are less likely to accept false information than if you proceed in the ordinary way, and you are more likely to find new combinations of known ideas. All in all, you risk very little and stand to gain a great deal by collaborating with your colleagues and managing beyond the ordinary.

The barriers to superior management can all be easily removed or gotten around, and you should deal with them early on. If they are ignored, they can delay acceptance and confuse what should be a simple process of evolution and improvement. When the barriers have been removed, managing beyond the ordinary makes practical sense and will be recognized as a better way to utilize the talents, skills, and energy of the people in your organization. You can make it fail-safe. There is no way you can lose by giving it a try.

5

Benefits of Managing Beyond the Ordinary

This is one of the shortest chapters in the book, not because the benefits of collaborating and managing beyond the ordinary are so few, but because they are so obvious. They hardly need to be stated.

The benefits of collaborating and managing beyond the ordinary are the same as the benefits of healthy living. If you treat your body well, give it good food and exercise and rest, it won't ache, and it will perform well for you. If you dump a lot of fats and junk food into it, smoke and drink to excess, never exercise, and cut your sleep short watching TV, your body won't perform as well as you want it to, and you won't feel as good as you think you should.

The body is a relatively closed system. A lot of things have an effect upon it, but what you put into it and how you treat it are major determinants of what you get from it in performance. If you take care of your body, it will take care of you, within its genetic limits. If you want high performance, feed and treat it well.

The same goes for management and decision making. Like a body, an organization is a relatively closed system. Put in poor resources and unreliable information, minimum thought and effort, disregard for the opinions and knowledge and abilities of others in the organization, inadequate planning, and disregard for what lies ahead, and you get poor decisions and lousy performance as a result. There is no way it can be otherwise.

If you want superior results from your organization, treat it as a top athlete treats her body: Put good ingredients into the hopper. Collaborate, and take advantage of others' good ideas. Manage beyond the ordinary. If you want superior resolutions to the problems that face you, manage to facilitate these events:

- Complete and accurate information is gathered about problems and is used in resolving them.
- Suggestions and information are drawn from sources who are close to the problems and know about them firsthand.
- All that is known about the problem is integrated through the best thinking of the best-informed and most experienced people available.
- The cause of the problem is determined and proved.
- The best ideas for the problem's resolution are gathered and organized.
- Those solutions that can be implemented at the lowest cost and the least inconvenience to the organization and that everyone can support and work with are generated from these ideas.
- Future problems and mistakes are anticipated, and actions are taken to avoid or prevent them.
- Recommendations for action are presented so that they can be fully understood and agreed to by those who have authority to implement them.

A List of Benefits

A number of benefits can be expected in companies that support managing beyond the ordinary. Among them are these:

- More reliable information is obtained about problems and better decisions are made about how to resolve them.
- Problems are resolved in less time and at lower cost than before.
- Fewer problems recur because they were dealt with adequately in the first place.

- Time and money are saved because problems don't have to be addressed over and over again.
- Managers feel more in control and less overwhelmed by an accumulation of unresolved problems.
- Everyone, from the CEO to the workers on the line, feels that progress is being made.
- Quality of product and service to customers are improved.
- Loyalty to the organization is increased.
- The stability, value, and future prospects of the organization are improved.
- People have a new way to contribute ideas and knowledge to help resolve problems that are important to them.
- People feel appreciated for what they know and can do and are accepted as valued members of the organization.
- People feel personal satisfaction at being able to share their ideas, knowledge, and skills.
- People are motivated to be more productive and to do higher quality work.
- People learn more about the objectives and values of the organization and its management.
- People feel responsible for the success of actions to which they have contributed.
- People take a greater interest in and responsibility for identifying and resolving future problems and issues.
- Turnover and waste are reduced, and the workspace becomes safer and cleaner.
- People learn a great deal from their collaborations.
- People who have learned how to collaborate on the job generalize these skills to other activities.
- Managers gain access to experience, knowledge, ideas, and information far beyond their own when they collaborate with their people.
- Managers are able to see their mistakes and make corrections before their errors become public.
- Managers are able to confirm their conclusions through collaboration before committing to action.
- Managers are able to delegate more authority and respon-

sibility to their subordinates, since everyone understands and uses the same approach.

- Skill at collaboration makes good managers better; they are more valued by the organization and more capable of managing difficult situations beyond the ordinary.

A List of Disadvantages

In spite of all its benefits, managing beyond the ordinary, like everything else, has its downside. Certain real disadvantages exist, and they must be considered. (Each can be reduced or eliminated by actions you can take, however.) Among the possible disadvantages are these:

- It takes effort to get collaboration going and to make managing beyond the ordinary happen—but you can start out at your own pace, do as much or as little as you want, with everything under your personal control, and feel your way into collaboration with a high degree of safety.
- You have to be sincere and honest with your subordinates, or they will think you are playing games—but you will come across as genuine if you ask them for their ideas, listen to what they say, and use their ideas in a productive way.
- You have to share the credit with your subordinates for good ideas generated and resolutions achieved—but you retain your individual achievement and competitive position as you do it, pointing to the excellent things your coworkers have done under your leadership, a point that will not be lost on your superiors.
- You have to develop a plan of action for yourself and your subordinates to accomplish the ten tasks—but you can all follow the ready-made procedure we have described, adapting it to your particular situation.

An Example of Beyond-the-Ordinary Managing

Does collaboration really work? Here is an example of a manager who faced a challenge and successfully dealt with it by enlisting the aid and wisdom of his colleagues.

A Plant Turnaround

Gene Summers was transferred to an agricultural product processing plant that was considered by the parent company to be in deep trouble and named general manager. The plant was old and dirty, and it had a high accident rate; its equipment was run down. There was labor unrest, productivity was low, and quality was barely acceptable. Many in the corporate office thought the plant should be shut down. The company president disagreed and said that there should be one last effort to turn it around. Summers was told that he would have one year and not much money to improve the plant.

When he arrived on the scene, he was appalled. Things were far worse than he had heard. He knew he couldn't handle the turnaround by himself, so he asked his managers and his supervisors to tell him what the problems were. After some hesitation, they did. He then asked his operators the same question. He got hundreds of problems in response, some big, some little, but all important to the people who had suggested them. He listed them on charts and posted them in the conference room so that he and his managers would see them every single day.

With his training director, Summers started a program that gave everyone a common procedure for resolving problems and let them use situations from the list as examples to practice on. When an individual or a group came up with a solution to a problem, he visited the work site and saw and heard the proposal for himself. He wrote short notes to everyone who helped resolve the problems and met with a different group of workers each week at noon—"Lunch With the Man," it was called—to hear their problems and ideas. He listened and learned and took action and by his interest gave encouragement to those who had given up hope that anything would ever improve.

Summers enlisted the workers' aid in correcting conditions in the plant. Some operators pointed out some loose railings that constituted a safety hazard. Summers said he didn't have money to hire someone to make repairs, but he would provide tools and materials if the operators could figure out how to fix it themselves. They came up with a cheap, efficient resolution and carried it out. Another group said that workers needed a dustfree place to leave their lunches and street clothes. When Summers provided plywood and hinges, they built lockers on their own time. A couple of supervisors got together and corrected a bottleneck in material flow that had slowed down the plant for years. Problem by problem, the troubles that had plagued the plant were eliminated and the issues crossed off the list.

One night, after the plant had shut down and everyone else had gone home, Summers walked through the plant. He found one of his notes framed above a maintenance mechanic's workbench. "Then I knew we had turned the corner," he said later. And indeed he had. The list of problems got shorter and shorter and finally disappeared. Absenteeism dropped, the accident rate fell off, productivity rose, and quality improved. "And the plant was clean. People picked up trash and swept the aisles and wiped down the equipment," he said. "It was their home now, a place they had a stake in. They took pride in this old, run-down wreck of a place they all said they hated a year ago."

The plant became profitable, and, instead of being shut down, it was enlarged. Labor problems fell off, and the satisfaction of the nearly seven hundred people who worked there increased tremendously. And Gene Summers? After two and a half years at that plant, he went on to manage a new division of the company. He went beyond the ordinary in the way he managed that worn-out processing plant, and going beyond the ordinary marked him as an extraordinary manager who deserved—and could handle—bigger and better things.

There is nothing new and untried about managing beyond the ordinary. Outstanding managers have been using these ideas for a long time. Julius Caesar, for example, was one of the most successful leaders known (until he was killed by political enemies who thought he had become a little too successful). In the introduction to her translation of Caesar's book, *The Civil War*, Jane Gardner has this to say about his leadership practices in 46 B.C.:

He succeeded in binding his men to him by strong ties of loyalty; he did this by making a point of close personal contact with small sections, if not with every individual, in the army. Particular instances of good service were noted and recalled when appropriate, and

he took pains to be acquainted with the centurions—
the company-sergeant-majors—of his legions, treating
them not merely as subordinates but as experienced
soldiers whose advice was to be heeded and respected.
This policy reaped its rewards.[1]

The importance of listening to his followers was lost on Na-
poleon, who thought he was infallible and marched on Moscow
in the winter, disregarding the advice of others who had been
there and knew the conditions he would face. Of more than a
hundred thousand soldiers who set out from France, fewer than
ten thousand returned.

The Bottom Line

Going beyond the ordinary, finding out a little more, asking for
advice and suggestions, thinking deeper and farther ahead, has
brought benefit to everyone who has tried it, as far as we know.
We don't know of anyone who has been hurt by making the
extra effort. It has worked for others, and we believe it will work
for you.

In our professional practice, we have seen scrap rates fall,
quality improve, absenteeism and turnover fall off, and productivity increase. These effects are worth money. We have also seen
people become more satisfied with the work they do, take pride
in their workspace and keep it clean, and become more concerned with resolving the problems facing their organization.
What is this worth? You decide.

Some of our clients have estimated the dollar value of the
results they obtained. One client said it saved $30 million; an-
other said it received a ten-dollar payback for every dollar spent
in learning the new procedures. We can't vouch for those figures
or say how they were obtained. They represent our clients' attempts to measure their bottom lines as a result of managing
beyond the ordinary. All we can say is that they believed and
accepted the figures as accurate.

Think about the how-to-do-it suggestions in Chapters 6
through 15 in terms of how you might apply the ideas in your

own job, and consider the concrete steps you might take to make your job easier and more productive. Select a problem or issue you will have to deal with, and put together a plan for resolving it on a small, easy scale. When the resolution is complete, step back and evaluate the results. What good came out of the effort? What could be improved the next time around? Then try the plan again. After all, what can you lose?

Note

1. Julius Caesar, *The Civil War*, transl. Jane P. Gardner (New York: Dorset Press, 1985).

SECTION TWO
The Ten Tasks

6
Task 1: Understanding the Situation vs. Leaping Directly Into Action

The first task that you must accomplish to manage beyond the ordinary is to understand the situation you are facing instead of leaping directly into action. Many managers say, "There's a problem. How are we going to fix it?" and then go directly into action. That's counterproductive. You need to find out as much as you can about the problem before doing anything—what its boundaries are, what major threats it poses, who or what is involved, what caused the problem, what questions you ought to be asking of whom.

You'd be surprised how many managers assume they know all they need to know in the first few minutes of being faced with a problem. They are so set on taking action that they can't see the point of checking to see if what they think they know is accurate. They think people are rewarded for doing things, not for asking a lot of questions, so they spring into action. They think they will find out whatever they don't already know as they go along, so why wait? They think decisive action is what the world rewards, missing the point that the *right* actions, not just any action, get applause.

What should you do? Form your working group with one or two other people who know about the problem and have a stake in it, and start finding out what's going on. It is much safer to assume from the start that the problem is more complex than you think. You don't know whether you are dealing with a tiger or a pussycat, so assume it is a tiger. If it turns out to be a pussycat, it is easy to simplify your approach. But if it turns out to be a tiger and you prepared for a pussycat, where are you?

Be a little cautious, and take your time. Ask questions, and find out what's happening. You'll make the time up later by knowing what you're doing. Ignorance poses a risk you don't need to take. You and your colleagues can avoid that risk by getting and sharing information and thinking your way through the situation until you are sure you all understand it in the same way.

Gathering Information by Degrees

Knowledge of what is going on with a problem situation comes by degrees. You never find out definitively what is happening on your first pass at gathering information, so make an extra effort to collect as much information as you can from different sources and different points of view. Then put it together in a coherent statement, and summarize it for your own benefit and for the benefit of whomever else may be involved. This is the base on which you will all build.

Making a summary statement of the problem is extremely important. Unless you put what you know into words, as accurately as you can, you have no way to work with others. Your statement of the situation becomes a rolling summary, one that changes and improves as new information comes in. It provides the up-to-date informational foundation for all you will do. When you have said, "This is what is going on," your co-workers can make useful contributions and correct errors, misinterpretations, and oversights. When they can "see" the problem, they can judge how complete and accurate your statement of it actually is.

SEEING THE REAL PROBLEM

A group of managers and engineers were trying to solve an urgent technical problem with an undersea weapons system. One engineer had drawn a diagram of the offending component on the blackboard. While the group was having coffee, a journeyman electrician walked by and saw the drawing. "That's not the way it is at all," he said, and he proceeded to change the diagram.

It turned out that a postinstallation fix had modified the system, since it wouldn't work properly as originally designed. Unfortunately, the engineer and, consequently the entire group, had been working with the original design, which was outdated. They would never have resolved the problem with the data they had. If they hadn't made their perception of the situation *visible* so that the person who really knew about the system could see the error in their information, they would still be there, wondering what was wrong and calling the problem "unsolvable." Summarizing, resummarizing, and making the information visible and open to inspection is the most productive thing any manager can do at this first stage in the process.

Breaking the Situation Apart

We tend to lump together problems that are in reality separate and should be considered apart. You may have a "personnel problem," a "production problem," or a "marketing problem," each of which comprises many individual problems and issues that have been joined under one general heading. You can resolve problems like these only after you have broken them apart and recognized the separate problems that make them up.

A statement like "The Baytown office has a personnel problem" tells you very little except where the problem is occurring and that it concerns people. When you have asked a number of questions and gotten answers from the people who know the details, you find that (1) a pay increase was promised the staff nine months ago but still hasn't come through, and nobody knows what is going on, (2) the heating and air conditioning system has broken down, and everyone has a headache, (3) two competing unions are battling for representation rights, and rumors have everyone in an uproar, (4) the office manager has an alcohol problem that is getting worse, and (5) the parking lot has been torn up during construction of the new research facility.

Now you can see the situation in a different light. It isn't all one problem but a tangle of problems, each of which must be considered as a separate issue for which separate actions may be taken. Some problems and issues may be interrelated, and some may not. But you can't make headway until you have taken the whole mess apart so that you can see its elements as separate concerns.

When you have broken the situation into its parts, you can begin to set priorities and concentrate on the most threatening and urgent problems first. Some issues will have serious consequences if they aren't dealt with now. Others have deadlines attached and demand immediate action. Still others can wait for a resolution. One of your most precious resources is time; setting priorities will help you get the most out of what little time you have.

Coming to a Shared Understanding

The purpose of Task 1 is to get the information out and visible, free of errors and misinterpretations, so that you and your people can understand it in common. If you share an understanding of a problem, you can deal with it together. If you don't all see the problem the same way, each of you will be trying to resolve a different concern, and that will get you nowhere. Task 1 isn't complete until all of you have agreed that your statement of the problems and issues is correct and that you can all work with it.

You use rational thinking in the first part of this task. You are collecting facts, learning about what has happened and what is going on. You are not drawing on experience, intuition, wisdom, or creative ability; these come into play later when you interpret and judge the information you have gathered and try to make sense of it. You start out with the facts, and nothing else, observe the immediate situation, and try to put it all together to form a picture of what is happening.

When you separate the situation into individual problems, you bring in your intuitive thinking, using your judgment, experience, wisdom, and gut feelings. You get the facts first, then arrange them in patterns that make sense to you, in light of what you know about the matter.

There will be no magic signal to tell you when you have

broken a situation down far enough. Your judgment will tell you when you have reduced a lump of intertwined problems to manageable proportions. When you can see each problem clearly, you have done enough. As runners say, "Listen to your body." When your gut tells you have gone far enough, stop and move on to the next task.

The same applies to setting priorities. Your judgment and experience will tell you that one issue is more important than another and has to be dealt with first. After you have identified the important matters, you need to test these conclusions against rational thinking. Do these priorities fit with the facts and make logical, practical sense? If they do, then you can think about them rationally, as you would any other hard data. But listen to your judgment in the beginning. If something tells you that one particular issue is important and needs immediate attention, listen. Ignoring your intuition could be a big mistake.

Forming a Working Group

As the mover, the responsible person, you may choose to begin resolving a simple problem by yourself. More likely, however, you will decide that you should involve a few others from the outset and will seek to involve a few other people who have direct knowledge and interest in the situation and who have a stake in seeing the problem resolved. These become your key people for this problem resolution. You will probably involve others later on in the process, but you and these people constitute the working group, the nucleus starting group.

This group needs to develop a shared understanding of the problem from the very beginning. The How-to-Do-It suggestions in this chapter and in the chapters that follow assume that you have arrived at such an understanding and have formed a working group. (If you decide to try and resolve the problem yourself, however, the suggestions we make apply to you as a working group of one.)

It's harder to do everything by yourself, and a lot more risky, but it can be done. Why is it more risky? Because you don't have someone else to challenge your line of thinking with another point of view. It's risky because you are less likely to discover new ideas and put together bits of information to create something that didn't exist before, and you are more likely to accept a resolution that is not as good as it might have been if you had drawn upon the experience and best ideas of others. But if you do decide to do it yourself, change the wording and ask yourself the questions you would otherwise ask other people.

One word of warning—if you do decide to form a group, you may be inclined to pick people who are geographically close to you for your working group because they are conveniently within reach and are people you know and have worked with before. Is that enough reason to select them? Do they really know that much about the situation, or are they merely handy? With telephone conference calls, e-mail, fax, and team computing, geographical proximity is no longer so important. Reach out for the best people for your working group, those who have direct knowledge of the problem and a stake in its resolution. It will make the difference between a so-so decision and an outstanding resolution.

Ask questions of your colleagues. You lead by asking questions. When you ask them a question, you get their immediate attention, direct them to the subject matter you want them to consider, and define the thinking task you want them to undertake. Nothing you can do as a leader is more effective than asking questions. If you tell the group members to do something, your orders are open to interpretation and subject to distortion in accordance with their biases and motivation. If you ask them a question, you draw them into your channel of thinking and define the boundaries of relevance for them. You also challenge them to come up with the best answers they can. People respond to questions that assume they know something worthwhile a lot better than they react to orders, so ask and ask again. You'll be surprised at the cooperation and results you obtain.

HOW TO DO IT

First, ask yourself this question: "Do I know everything about this problem situation that I need to know?" If you can honestly answer yes, go on to the next task, but if there is any doubt in your mind, stop here and ask questions of others. Get a few people who know about the problem as a working group, and find out what is going on. Follow these steps, adapted as necessary to your situation:

1. *Set the task.*
   "The first thing we have to do is find out what the problem is and what's going on here."
   You have to tell the people in your working group what the task is: to get the information out so that everyone can understand the problem the same way.

2. *Get the information out.*
   "Here is the situation as I know it at this time."
   Describe it in enough detail so that your people know what you're talking about, but don't overwhelm them. Then ask:
   "What do you know about it?"
   Let them tell it their way. Their accounts may ramble and contain inconsistencies or contradictions. Don't worry about that now. Get the information out and on the table. Be prepared to ask follow-up questions to keep the information coming.
   "And then what happened?"
   "Tell me more about that."

3. *Develop a statement of the problem.*
   When all the information seems to be in, try to summarize it in a simple, clear statement.
   "Here's what I think the situation is."
   Ask for additions, corrections, or changes.
   "Is there anything you can add to, correct, or change in what I said?"
   Update and modify your statement of the problem to accommodate new information. You are still trying to get the facts straight. Rephrase your statement until there are no further suggestions or changes. Restate the problem in its final form. Write your statement on a board or flip chart so that everyone can see it. This will help all of you recognize errors.

4. *Break the problem apart and separate issues.*
   Draw on the group's knowledge, judgment, and experience. Ask whether this is a single problem or whether it should be broken into a number of separate problems and issues.
   "Are we dealing with several problems here? Let's see if we can't break this apart into smaller chunks."
   Draw out comments. List subproblems and issues so that everyone can see them. Be prepared to ask questions to keep the ideas moving.
   "What did you mean by that?"
   Invite others to express their opinions, make additions or corrections, or rephrase earlier statements.
   "Do we need to break this situation down further?"
   Make a separate corrected summary statement of each problem and issue as you now understand it.

5. *Set priorities.*
   "Which of these is most important and should be dealt with first?"
   Discuss relative seriousness, time pressure, and likely consequences if each problem or issue is not resolved now.
   Assign priorities—high, medium, or low.
   Get agreement on the priorities.

6. *Get agreement and commitment on the problems and issues.*
   "Are these accurate statements of the problems and issues that we must resolve?"
   Get positive agreement. Question directly anyone who doesn't say, "Yes, I can agree with each one." Draw out and incorporate any new information. When you have agreement, restate problems and issues to be sure you have them right.
   "Then these are the problems and issues we will work on together."

Summary

Task 1 is to develop clearly understood statements of the problems and issues that everyone will work together to resolve. To complete this task, gather a few people who have a stake in the problem to form a working group, then ask questions and lead the discussion to dig out the information you need. You will need to go through this sequence of actions:

1. Set the task.
2. Get the information out.
3. Develop a statement of the problem.
4. Break the problem apart and separate issues.
5. Set priorities.
6. Get agreement and commitment.

When you have completed this first basic task, you will have built a foundation of information and understanding on which to construct your problem resolution. You will need more information as you go along, but you will add that new information to what you already have. After completing Task 1, you will know what you have to deal with and what information you have to work with. Next you must determine exactly what your purpose is, where you want to go, and what you want to get done.

7

Task 2:
Clarifying Your Real
Purpose vs. Doing
the Same Old Thing

Task 2 in managing beyond the ordinary requires clarifying your real purpose instead of doing the same old thing. You have to identify and understand what your real purpose is and what you hope to achieve, or else there is no reason to believe you will ever successfully accomplish it.

It is easy to assume that the purpose you have had in the past needs no adjustment, that the only problem you have is with the means you are using to achieve that purpose. When something doesn't work very well, you fix up whatever seems to be wrong, make it as good as it was before, and continue on. That way, you don't have to think. When it breaks down or gives you trouble once more, you simply patch it up again. It's only when someone gets tired of this routine and asks, "What are we trying to get done here?" that you can hope to break out of the rut and find improvement.

A CASE IN POINT: TACKLING THE PAPERWORK JUNGLE

Ed Boyd, a manager for one of our clients, moved into a new position in a division of the company. The paperwork jungle was there to meet him, just as it had bogged down his predecessors. In the past, people had made the paper mill turn faster and had stream-lined some forms, increasing efficiency somewhat. But Boyd didn't settle for the way it had always been. He asked the magic question "What are we really trying to get done here?" The answer was easy: "Be productive, do our jobs, and generate no more red tape and paperwork than we have to."

At every meeting he had with his staff, Boyd would hold up another report. "Do any of you need this? Would it cripple your operation if you didn't have it?" A surprising number of times the response was a resounding "No!," and the report would be discon-tinued. Sometimes one or two people said that they used the report, while others didn't. Boyd would then limit distribution to those who needed it. Sometimes he found that several reports could be com-bined. Other times he found that only a few items of information in a report were used, so he streamlined the report's contents. In six months, he had reduced the paperwork to less than half of what it had been and substantially increased his unit's productivity.

If Boyd hadn't asked the right question, nothing would have changed. But he asked what the true objectives and purposes of all this reporting were and then asked if there wasn't a better way to achieve them. He wasn't forced to ask the question by circum-stances, but he saw a problem and voluntarily chose to deal with it. He pushed the envelope and redesigned his organization; he went beyond the ordinary. He could have made the old system work a little faster, but he chose instead to set a new standard and to find a better way of realizing it.

Finding the Real Purpose

Some organizations progress steadily, day by day, while others stand still or move ahead only by fits and starts. Wonder how the steady ones do it? Progress is directly correlated to the num-ber of times this question is asked: "What are we really trying to get done here? Is there a better way?" A lot of modest improve-ments keep you moving ahead and in the long run win the race. Relying on the big breakthrough, the great inspiration or innovation, is risky because you never know when or if it is going to occur.

The best strategy, of course, is to combine the two, to resolve lots of little, run-of-the-mill problems and also make the big breakthroughs. Luckily, you can, because they go together. What you learn by making modest improvements is more likely to stimulate a major breakthrough than just hoping for one. You simply can't lose by constantly asking, "What are we really trying to get done here?" You may find that you started out to deal with a medium-size problem and found the answer to a huge, more important one without even looking for it.

There has been much interest in reengineering or reinventing corporations,[1] that is, reorganizing corporate activities so that a weakness or a problem can be eliminated or avoided. The same thinking can apply to the reengineering of management.[2] It starts with an examination of purpose, judging whether existing goals adequately reflect the needs of the corporation. Taking a fresh view enables you to see both the purpose you are trying to achieve and the means you are using to achieve it from a new perspective and thus to pick up on any problem or imbalance between the two and do something to improve matters.

Are there always other and better means to achieve an objective? Sometimes there are, and you can find them if you look. But not always. If you step back and ask the necessary questions and find that you are doing what you should be doing, then there's no need to change this aspect of the business. Good! Look at another aspect, and then another. The point is that every time you see or suspect a problem, ask the question "Is this what we *ought* to be doing?" There are more inadequate actions out there than you suspect. And you don't have to reengineer the whole corporation, either. You can improve and redesign individual situations and activities at any level.

The sharper, the more relevant, and the more challenging your purpose, the better your performance will be, because you'll be able to recognize when the means you are using are ineffective or inefficient. If you have only a foggy notion of what you are trying to accomplish, you won't be able to see when you are doing a poor job. Whatever you do, don't settle for doing the same old thing over and over. Look at each problem that comes up, and ask if there is an opportunity to do it better. Chances are you'll find something to improve. You can be absolutely sure you won't find anything if you don't look.

Using All Modes of Thinking

All modes of thinking are appropriate for this task, and you should make sure that you and your co-workers use them all. You have no idea where a better idea will come from. Maybe it's right there in front of you, and you can uncover it by asking questions. Maybe it's something you learned at another time and place. Perhaps it's an idea that will just pop out of your memory. Maybe you and someone else can put your ideas together and create something new. You never know. If you open up all possible channels and appeal to all the ways of thinking, you have a good chance of uncovering an important new idea.

To question purpose, your first move should be to establish clearly what the present purpose is. "What are we trying to accomplish by doing it this way?" Don't be surprised if people haven't thought about it. When you and your people have defined the present purpose, you can then ask if this is what you should be doing or if another purpose should be explored. In Boyd's case, the old purpose had been to get all the reports through in the shortest time possible. When he asked the question, he realized the purpose should be to get the *useful* information through, which made a big difference.

When you ask your people for their opinion of the present purpose, it may pay off immediately. They will shift to their intuitive thinking, based upon years of experience. "I've always thought that was a dumb thing to try to do!" someone says. Ask questions to find out why that person thinks it's stupid and then ask them what the *ideal* goal or purpose should be. Never mind that some people will say, "That's too hard, and we can't do it." Set the objective and see how it might be reached.

We knew a manager who would pick out an operation he would like to see speeded up, then ask his manufacturing people what problems they would have doing it in three hours instead of five. "Can't do it," they'd say. "There would be this problem and this one and this one. . . ." Then he would focus on the first problem they named and ask, "What would you have to do to solve this one?" They would think about that and come up with a resolution. Then he would focus on the next, and the next, until all the problems had been resolved. By upgrading the standard—the purpose at the problem level—then challenging his people to meet it, he created one of the most efficient operations in the industry. His gut feeling would tell him there was an improvement that was needed. Then he would get his people to switch to rational thinking and logic to achieve something better than they might have done without his questions.

The purpose of Task 2 is to shake you and your people out of whatever ruts you may have fallen into. You're in a rut when you think what you have been doing is good enough for now. Get out of the rut by looking around and asking, "What are we trying to get done?" Then redesign, reinvent, reengineer, and lift your organization to a higher level of performance.

Another Kind of Purpose: Collaboration

There is another kind of rut many people fall into. That is the rut of constant competition, of always thinking in terms of "my side winning out over the other side," instead of "Let's do what is best for all of us." You need to state the purpose of working and thinking together early in your search for a resolution if you expect collaboration to occur.

You do it by defining it as a ground rule: "We need to put together the best ideas that all of us have and come up with a better resolution than any of us might think up alone." It's likely they'll say, "Oh sure, yes," and that will be all you need to say. They know what thinking and working together is, although they may never have used the word "collaboration." Once you mention it, they will stop being competitive and start working together. You may have to remind them along the way, but once you begin to ask for their ideas and listen to what they say, you will have little trouble. You will have set a new purpose and a new pathway to follow, and they will accept it completely once they see what you mean and that you are committed to it.

HOW TO DO IT

First, ask your working group, "Do we know what we are trying to accomplish here, and is that what we should be trying to achieve?" If you can honestly answer yes on both accounts, go on to the next task, but if there is any doubt, stop and consider your purpose in detail. You will also want to establish that your purpose as a group is to collaborate and not to compete, to put your best ideas together to develop a better resolution you can all support.

1. *Set the task.*
   "We have to make sure that what we are trying to correct or improve is what we should be doing in the first place."
   This tells your people the task is to think about what the purpose is, to be clear about the objective of the thing or action you have a problem with.

2. *Get out ideas about the purpose.*
   "What is the purpose of this thing or action we are concerned with improving?"
   Focus on the thing or action as you know it now. Get at the basic reason for its being done. Be prepared to nudge the group along with follow-up questions.
   "Why do we do this at all?"
   "Could you say more about that?"

3. *Evaluate the present purpose.*
   "Does this purpose say what we're really trying to get done, or can we state a better one?"
   Get the group to think through what a more adequate definition of purpose would be, how the present one might be improved.
   "What's wrong with the present purpose?"
   "What do you think would make it more complete?"

4. *Make a better statement of the purpose.*
   "What do you think the best statement of purpose for this thing or action would be?"
   Get the group's ideas about a better purpose or objective. Combine ideas where possible. Let the new statement set a higher standard of performance.
   Arrive at the best statement of the purpose possible, and get shared understanding and agreement of the improved purpose.

Summary

Task 2 requires that you arrive at a shared understanding of the goal you hope to achieve. Ask your colleagues what your purpose is and whether that is what you really want done in the first place. If that isn't good enough, what would an improved statement of purpose be? You will go through these steps:

1. Set the task.
2. Get out ideas about the purpose.
3. Evaluate the present purpose.
4. Make a better statement of the purpose.

You have collected a foundation of information about the problem and looked carefully at what you are trying to get done. Next, you have to anticipate what additional information you will need, identify the people who have it, and decide how you can get them to share it with you.

Notes

1. Michael Hammer and James Champy, *Reengineering the Corporation* (New York: HarperBusiness, 1993).
2. James Champy, *Reengineering Management* (New York: HarperBusiness, 1995).

8

Task 3: Determining What You Need to Know and Who Knows It vs. Doing It Yourself

Involving the people who know about the problem instead of trying to solve it yourself is Task 3 in managing beyond the ordinary. You have to reach out to your resource people to find out who knows what you need to know in order to resolve the problem successfully and then get those people to collaborate with you.

Three Choices in Problem Resolution

To resolve any problem, you have three choices: (1) you can deal with it yourself, (2) you can involve a lot of other people, or (3) you can be highly selective and involve only those who know the most about it and can help you find the best resolution possible.

We've said it before: It's risky to deal with a complex problem by yourself. If you choose the first option, the things you don't know may later turn out to be important. When you go it alone, you are depending on what you know, the experience you've had, and your own judgment, and you must hope that your view of the situation is correct. Furthermore, if you don't get others to carry some of the load for you, you'll also end up doing a tremendous amount of work. This isn't a good choice unless you want to live dangerously.

The second choice suggests that you open the problem up and involve a lot of other people, making sure that every possible group and interest is represented. In this option, you let in everyone who shows any interest, and if you have any doubts about someone's interest, you invite him anyway. After all, people like being involved, don't they? Not really. Whoever said that never spent hours in a conference room where too many people had too little to say and took too long to say it. Nothing irritates a good person more than wasting time while the talk goes around and around to no end. You want sharp thinkers who will bring worthwhile knowledge to the table, not people who will impede progress rather than contribute to it.

The best option is the third choice—selectively bringing in those who know and can give you the most help. How do you find these people? Not around the water cooler. They are busy, out where things are getting done. You will have to reach out for them, and you will have to convince them that it is in their interest to make some of their scarce time available to you.

Start off by assuring them that they won't have to spend a lot of time in useless meetings. Respect their scheduling and time pressures. Use the phone, conference calls, fax, e-mail, and team computing software to go to them, rather than always making them come to you physically. Let them see that you are dealing with a specific, limited, defined problem and not an open-ended matter that will go on and on. When you do require a meeting, keep it focused and concise. When they see that you mean business about a problem they know and are concerned with, they will cooperate.

Determining What You Need to Know and Who Knows It

To begin deciding whom to involve, think through what you need to know. If you start out with a list of people, you will end up with the same old boys' or girls' network, the people you most often see. If you start out with a list of what you need to know, however, you will assemble a group of experts who have the specific information you require, some of whom you may not even know. Think answers, not personalities.

It's easy to do this. In the introduction we described the plant manager at Beta Corporation, who was told to cut his labor costs and increase production and who decided to install robots as part of the solution. He spent hours thinking about the project before he made any moves. He thought through the information he would need in order to be successful and sought answers to these questions:

- What areas of the operation would enjoy the greatest gains in labor efficiency from the introduction of robots?
- What operations would the robots have to perform in order to be successful?
- How would the robots be integrated into the assembly line?
- How would the robots have to be operated and maintained in order to realize the mandated gains in efficiency?
- What problems would have to be avoided for the robots to succeed?

These are all practical questions. The people who do and manage the work are most likely to know the answers to them. So the plant manager ended up with several groups of resource persons—experienced production specialists, supervisors, machine operators, and foremen. No theorists, philosophers, or professional meeting-attenders; just the people who would be most likely to know about the problem at hand and contribute good ideas. What could be simpler than that?

The plant manager retained control of the process throughout. The groups designed the robots, drawing on their knowledge of the job, and tested them out in prototype form. The manager listened carefully to their ideas because they knew more about what had to be done than he did. When he had studied and approved their recommendations, he brought in outside engineers and manufacturing people to produce the finished hardware and to turn their good ideas into reality. He then had the people who had designed the robots in the first place take over their installation and operation.

The plant manager thus had the people who knew the most about the problem create what was, in their judgment, the best resolution, which they then passed on to him as their recommendation. With responsibility for the project, he made his own decisions, utilizing their input as he saw fit. And it worked, because the best minds available for that problem had collaborated with him to produce the best resolution possible within that situation and under those conditions. He didn't risk anything, and he gained a great deal. The resolution he recommended to his top management was much better than anything he could have created by himself.

Determining Whom You Should Involve and How to Get Them to Cooperate

The people you need to involve in your problem resolution are in the organization and in the world beyond. All you have to do is recognize them and invite them in. There are four common-sense criteria for deciding whom you should involve:

1. *Those who know the most about the problem and have had firsthand experience with it.* These people will have the most practical suggestions about what has caused the problem and what will set it right. They are the memory of your organization, holding recollections of earlier problems faced and resolved and what was learned from them, a resource you cannot afford to ignore or underuse.

2. *Those who will bear responsibility for implementing the resolution and must make it succeed.* Their ideas will be down-to-earth because they know they will have to make them work. If the resolution contains impractical, hard-to-implement actions that have been forced on your workers, they won't do much to make those ideas succeed. Workers are a reservoir of ideas that will make successful implementation a lot easier.

3. *Those who can be champions for the resolution, have a personal interest in its success, and will use their influence to see it implemented.* You need a champion who will fight for your resolution, be sure it gets a fair hearing, and push for its implementation. If you and your colleagues develop a good resolution but nothing changes, then your efforts will have been a waste of time. A champion with clout and a stake in the outcome can make things happen. Recruit a champion for insurance.

4. *Those who know how to work together with others to arrive at recommendations that all can accept and support.* You need people in the first three categories who can and will work together to achieve a resolution you can all agree on and support. Some people, however, are loners and find it hard to work with others; some are so contrary and confrontational that they can't agree with anyone else about anything. There is a minimum skill and desire that all must have, or the project will founder. This does not mean that you should pick only people who agree with everything you say. You should avoid the me-too contingent, since all they will give you is an echo of what you already know. You need new ideas from people who will join their own ideas with the ideas of others to create a solution that nobody would have produced alone.

You find the people who meet these requirements by asking for them. Once you know what kind of information you need, you can ask someone familiar with the subject area to recommend likely prospects. They'll tell you, "See Ralph. He knows more about that than the rest of us put together."

A manager about to involve others in a problem resolution should pull together the best group of informed resource people possible. A manager can do that because she has full control over who and how many will take part. The people should be experienced, respected for their knowledge, and able to work together. There should be no weak or surplus individuals.

Logistics and Other Practical Matters

Group size is an immediate concern in any undertaking. The rule should always be to have the bare minimum of people to do the job and not one person more. Have the smallest group feasible to get the information you need, from both users and implementers, plus a champion.

Selection controls quality. Pick the people who can give you the most and who can reach others who may have additional information you want. Let them gather the information, integrate it, and pass it on to you and the rest of your co-workers. Let them also communicate outward from you to their constituents. You can get much of the information you need by phone, fax, e-mail, or team computing network, as well as by casual one-on-one contacts. A few carefully selected people can bring in a lot of answers. You are striving to locate the *right information*, not the most information. You don't want a series of formal meetings that waste your resource people's time. Think of the most efficient and least disruptive ways you can get the information you need. That is only common courtesy and will be much appreciated by the people you deal with.

KEEPING A CONTROVERSIAL PLAN AFLOAT

Tom Keebler was chosen to create a harbor development plan for an East Coast seaport community. The issue was highly political, with five very different factions involved: the town businesspeople, a large group of prosperous retirees from outside the area, another large group of yacht and pleasure-boat owners, middle-class commerical fishermen, and a large number of poor fishermen. The goal of the project was to develop a plan that would fairly serve the interests of everyone. Other plans had been proposed before and always ended in hostility and a polarization of the five factions. Harbor development was considered a virtually impossible task, but it needed to be done, and so another attempt was undertaken.

Keebler considered the information he would need and then selected one knowledgeable representative from each faction, plus a senior person from the town council, to make up his working group. He brought the six people together first to determine the characteristics of an ideal plan for the harbor and what it should do for the people of the community. Through these spokespersons, the views of the various parties were expressed. He then held a town meeting where the characteristics of the ideal plan were presented and discussed, and suggestions were contributed from the audience. There was no discussion of the specific actions that might be taken; the only topic was the objectives to be served by whatever actions might be considered later on.

These objectives were stated as a set of criteria that was reviewed and agreed to in a second public meeting. Everyone accepted the objectives of the project and became committed to creating a practical plan that would convert these objectives into reality.

Keebler and his team developed a plan that met the established criteria, using input from each faction provided by its representative on the working group. Elements of the plan were then communicated outward to all the factions through the same representatives, and suggestions and new ideas were brought back in for incorporation in the draft plan. A final plan was drawn up and unanimously approved in a third public meeting, and soon after it was implemented. No group got everything it wanted, but each group got a lot of what it felt was important. The project was judged fair by everyone involved, and everybody pulled together to make it work.

Not many people spent time on the project. The working group, consisting of seven members, including the chairman, met in nine two-hour meetings. The five representatives of the factions, who had firsthand knowledge of their constituents' special problems, acted as conduits for information. The group gathered ideas from many sources, reaching some by telephone and some by mail; most ideas, however, came from just talking around, something the group members would have done anyway.

The member from the town council became the group's champion. She was enthusiastic and personally concerned with the future of the harbor because she lived close to it. She supported the group's recommendations to the rest of the community. In fact, each of the group's members had a personal stake in the plan and understood that for the plan to succeed, everyone must win, not just one faction. So the groups collaborated, in spite of politics and long-held special-interest positions, to produce a plan that everyone could support.

Perhaps 250 people contributed to the harbor project, yet there were only nine meetings of the seven members and three public sessions to present recommendations and receive suggestions.

Everyone felt involved because everyone's ideas were listened to
and used. An inclusive approach and careful organization of both
people and information made the difference.

Picking Your Team

Choosing the people to work with you requires that you use
your intuitive thinking. The decision is subjective and is based
on your experience with these and other people in the past.
There is no objective, rational yardstick you can use to decide
whom to recruit, and your gut can tell you things your head
cannot.

Picking people to collaborate with you is different from hir-
ing new employees. You are asking people to cooperate with
you and share what they know about a specific problem and to
work with you as equals for this purpose, regardless of their
status in the company and their job titles. You are asking them
to share because they are qualified by knowledge and experience and are your peers with respect to this problem. You are
asking for the participation of their knowledge, and nothing
more.

You can judge what people know about the problem and
how well you think they can work with others on the basis of
your experiences with them and the reports of others. You can
also evaluate their concern for the problem and their wish to see
it set right. You need not document why and how you decide or
fill out personnel forms. If you make a mistake—and you usually won't—you simply thank them for their time and ask someone else.

Motivating the Group

How do you motivate your colleagues to work together? You
pick people who are already familiar with the problem, think it
is important, and care about it. If they aren't motivated by their
knowledge and interest in the problem, they aren't the people
you want working with you. Good people already have ideas

and opinions they want to share with someone; more than any-thing else, they want to find someone who will listen to those ideas. So that is how you motivate them: You find the people who have ideas and experience, who care about the problem and are already motivated to do something about it, and you listen to them and seriously consider what they have to contribute.

Did you ever ask someone for an opinion about something important to her and find that she didn't have anything to tell you or didn't want to talk about it? It doesn't happen very often. The fact that you recognize someone for her ideas is motivating by itself. The fact that you listen keeps her going. You want to share what you know with people who will respect your ideas and give them a chance. So does the other guy. Motivation is not much of a problem if you pick people who have ideas and are honestly interested in what they have to say. Being listened to carefully is all the reward most people want.

How do you start the information flowing? You simply ask for it. You describe the problem and say you think that the group has some ideas about it. Then you ask for members' thoughts about whatever you want to know. It's as easy as that. People are proud of what they know, and they're proud to be able to help you. If you are honest with them and give them the respect they deserve, they will be glad to share whatever they know.

Sometimes, however, they can't. After all, you're trying to recruit the people who know the most, and they're usually the busiest because they are in demand. They may not have time, or they may have some conflict of interest that gets in the way. Don't take it personally and think there's something wrong with you. They will know who else is well informed and will refer you to other people who can help. If they don't have time to meet with you, maybe they will dash off a fax or e-mail note if you ask for it.

It is even easier to recruit and motivate your champion. You select someone who has influence and who is already interested in the problem you want to resolve. Your champion has been frustrated because nothing has been done about an issue that he considers important. You say, "We are going to resolve a prob-lem that has been bugging you. Will you help us?" Then you provide the information that will help your champion move your ideas along and look good at the same time.

The purpose of this task is to enlist the help of the best people you can find for your problem. It takes a little diplomacy, but success in getting the people you want comes mainly from showing that you are serious and will do an honest job in dealing with a problem situation they think is important.

HOW TO DO IT

Ask yourself, "Are the people who know and care about this problem sufficiently involved in its resolution?" If the answer is yes, go on to the next task. But if you think the resolution might gain from the ideas of others, you and your working group should think through what you will have to know and who has that information. Then reach out and enlist the aid of those who have the answers. You orient your working group by following this outline:

1. *Set the task.*
   "What information do we need, and who has it?"
   This tells your co-workers that the task is to determine the answers you need and who can give them to you and should therefore be involved.

2. *Identify the information you need.*
   "What do we need to find out?"
   Conduct a census of the general information you will need, specific details to come later.
   "What other aspects of the problem do we need to know about?"
   Survey the entire situation, and consider what you need to know. Probe to make sure you have thought of everything.
   "Have we missed anything?"

3. *Identify who has the answers.*
   "Who will give us the best information on this?"
   Let your group think of the quality of the answers it should get, then think of the best sources.
   "Who else knows a lot about this?"

4. *Determine how to get the information.*
   "How can we get these people to help us?"

Get suggestions about how to approach and catch the resource persons' interest and how to show them how they will benefit. Find out how to use the resource persons with the least inconvenience to them.

5. *Recruit a champion.*
"Whom can we get to fight for us and push our ideas?"
Your group will have good suggestions for a champion. Show how the person will benefit from your resolution.

6. *Plan for information gathering and integration.*
"Who will gather what information, and how will we put it all together?"
Decide who will do what and when and how you will integrate the information after you have gathered it. Develop a strategy for getting and sharing information.

Summary

Task 3 is to determine what information you will need and whom you will get it from. You get the people in your working group to think about who should be involved by asking questions and following these six steps:

1. Set the task.
2. Identify the information you need.
3. Identify who has the answers.
4. Determine how to get the information.
5. Recruit a champion.
6. Plan for information gathering and integration.

You know what the problem situation and purpose is and have resource people ready and willing to help you find the best resolution possible. The preliminaries are over. Now you're ready to define and describe the problem in hard, accurate, specific terms. That is Task 4.

9

Task 4: Getting the Complete Story About the Problem vs. Settling for a General Account

Task 4 in managing beyond the ordinary is getting the complete story about the problem instead of settling for a general account of it. You have to determine—in accurate, specific terms—*exactly* what the problem is, with no generalities and no vague statements. You must ask, "In hard, objective, specific terms, what is our problem? What is the complete story?"

The Problems of Telling the Complete Story

The average person is not very good at telling the complete story; descriptions of what happened usually come out in general terms, not in specifics, and in pieces that have to be fitted together. Why? Because we go from an unorganized memory of images of events that occurred through time and space to a description in words that has to make sense to someone who can't see those images.

Even though we can see what took place in our visual memory, telling what happened is a complex task in which we translate forms and feelings into a few words culled from our inventory of thousands. We use general terms and collapse a tremendous amount of rich detail into a few cold phrases. That seems all right to us, because we can still see what the words represent. But to the listener, who doesn't have the visual details as backup, it leaves out a great deal.

We could describe what we know more accurately if we only knew in advance which details were important. If we had some guide that would tell us, "This is essential, never leave it out!," we would always include the crucial material and skip the rest. But we don't. So we try to summarize what we know and end up giving an incomplete account. Read any detective mystery or any news story about a crime, and you'll find that details were dropped, left out, or unrecognized, only to become important later on.

Real life is more frustrating than fiction. A police officer at an accident asks the owner of the damaged car what happened, and the driver tells him that he was hit broadside on the right by a guy in a Chevrolet coming from the left who went through a stop light. How could you be hit on the right by a car from the left? The driver, it turns out, was making a U-turn when the Chevy plowed into him. After more questions, it turns out that the car was blue and going at least thirty miles per hour and a wreck, maybe ten years old. Four doors or two? Oh, two—a pickup. By putting it all together, the officer slowly builds a picture of what happened.

Why bother with all those facts? Because the officer has to identify a specific vehicle and a specific driver as causing the damage, out of all the vehicles and drivers who could have done it. One driver did it, and one alone, in an old blue Chevy pickup, coming through a red light from the left at considerable speed. The policeman will need all of that and more, specific and precise, if he is to understand what happened. To prove who did it, the officer will have to match details of the cause (the pickup and the way it was driven) with details of the effect (the accident and the damage to the other car) with a high degree of accuracy.

The same thing occurs with business problems. Elements come together to constitute a cause, and this cause matches exactly the effect it has produced. To find the cause, you start with the effect, just as the officer started with the accident and the bashed-in car. You then reconstruct the sequence of events until you arrive at a cause, a complex of elements, that explains all the effects you have observed. You get a match between the cause and the result it produced—the complete story. You find the cause by matching patterns, and the better you recognize and understand the details of the effect, the more likely you are to recognize the unique cause that brought it about. In business, the effect is called a problem.

Almost everything in business is about performance, getting things done. You produce or arrange something and expect it to perform in a certain way. If it doesn't, you have a problem. It doesn't meet the standards you set for it, you see a deficiency in its performance. Some flaw caused that deficiency. Understanding the effect and its cause will help you correct the deficiency and get things back on track.

Suppose that your company performs a service. You expect your customers to be satisfied with that service. They aren't, and you hear complaints. The deficiency in service is the problem, as evidenced by the complaints, and you will have to backtrack to find the cause. You start with the complaints to find out what aspect of the service performed poorly; you then seek out what caused the breakdown so that you can correct the problem. Some of the details will be critical to your understanding of the problem, and a lot more will not. Task 4 is getting the most precise, accurate, and specific portrait of the effect you can possibly get. You will need this information if you are to track down the cause of the problem.

Drawing a Portrait of the Problem

In his book *The Elephant's Child,* Rudyard Kipling described the process of drawing a portrait with words as well as anyone ever has. Kipling was an outstanding reporter and a storyteller beyond compare. He knew how to present a complete picture of whatever had happened. His formula has been repeated in journalism texts for a hundred years; it has been elaborated on, but the basic method remains as he said it:

> *I keep six honest serving men,*
> *They taught me all I know,*

Their names are WHAT and WHY and WHEN
And HOW and WHERE and WHO.

We ask questions, we get answers. Depending on the quality of the questions, the answers are either helpful or useless. If we take Kipling's questions, change their order slightly, and sharpen their wording to fit better in the business world, we have a guide for describing any problem, of any content, anywhere, any time, in precise terms. The questions become our key to identifying the details that will lead us to the cause of the problem.

Describing the faulty outcome requires answering—with specifics—questions such as these:

• *Deficiency:* What's *wrong?* What's the *defect?* What performance is not the way it should be or doesn't come up to standard? If you make a product with a panel that should be smooth but it has a scratch on it, that is a deficiency; something is wrong. Suppose you collect information on a form, and one item has not been completed. That is a deficiency. A salesperson's failure to give the right information to a customer is another deficiency. Whatever its nature, the performance deficiency needs to be described in full detail if the problem is going to be understood and resolved.

• *What.* What object, action, procedure, or condition is affected? For the scratch, it's on the panel. Which panel? The right-hand panel. What form was not completed? The 1040. What information wasn't given correctly to the customer by the salesperson? How to get a refund if not satisfied. What *thing* are we talking about? The object or thing that has suffered the deficiency needs to be described in full detail.

• *Who.* People are part of almost every problem, so we must identify the people involved in the situation—who they are, by name and function and relevant characteristics. They may be players and doers, the receivers of actions, or merely bystanders. Joe may have harassed Marilyn, as witnessed and reported by Jane and Ellen. Identify everyone involved.

• *Where.* Where in geographical space was the deficient performance seen or reported? What location? Everything is somewhere; nothing is everywhere or nowhere. Describe exactly where the problem was seen or encountered.

- *Where on the Object.* Where is the defect on the object? The scratch is in the upper left corner of the right-hand panel. The incomplete documentation on the 1040 form was on lines 23a and 23b. The gap in the information given the customer was in the sales presentation. Locate exactly where the trouble is.

- *When.* When in clock or calendar time did the problem occur? Everything occurs precisely at some time. There is no such thing as "no" time or "about" time. Determine the time as exactly as you can; knowing the time will help establish the relationship between this problem and other occurrences.

- *When in the Sequence.* When in the sequence of events did the problem occur? Time flows in a stream, so everything happens as part of a sequence of events. It was after this and before that (e.g., after painting and before assembly). Fixing the problem's position in a sequence of acts also helps you establish relationships between this and that.

- *Unique Features.* What's unique, unusual, different, or remarkable about the deficiency? What catches your attention? It may be an unusual distribution or appearance or presence; a smell or feel or color; a sound or texture; or a size or dimension or number. It may be a unique, seemingly "unrelated" effect or a change or a modification, or what appears to be a coincidence. If it's unusual and surprises you, it probably doesn't belong and is important. Ask about it and follow up. It may lead you to something you weren't aware of before.

The last category, "Unique Features," requires an explanation. It refers to characteristics that catch our eye. In the context of problems, unique features are details that stand out because they are unusual or different or surprising in some way; they make something in our brain go "Oh-oh" when we see them. They are details that don't fit with our expectations, like the sharp smell of an electrical overload or a vibration that develops in a piece of machinery or an abrupt change in a pattern of behavior.

You may not be consciously aware of what it is that catches your attention. It may be subtle and just barely there, but it makes you pause for a moment and try to locate it. These discrepancies usually turn out to be significant and give you a clue as to what caused the deficiency. They should always be noted and followed up for an explanation. If you say, "That's curious," but then go on and forget about the incident, you may have turned your back on the cause.

We have expanded considerably on five of Kipling's questions and added one of our own, Unique Features. Did we forget his Why? Not on your life! That is the subject of Chapter 10. Before we get to it, however, we want to consider something important that Kipling did not include in his rhyme but knew about and used in his story telling—the "But not . . ." side of the tale. The "But not . . ." side of any story adds drama and helps one find the answer to Why.

The "But Not" Question

When you draw the portrait of a problem, you are trying to make its outlines as accurate as you can, because pattern recognition relies on our seeing boundaries or outlines. Boundaries are the lines that separate what we observe that *Is* the problem from that which lies outside *But Is Not* part of it. The But Not question sets up a contrast at once.

A client manufactured four models of a household appliance and distributed them through many retail channels. People in the field reported to the product manager that they were getting serious quality complaints. The product manager narrowed down the problem when he found out the complaints were with the *finish* But Not with the mechanism, on *Model A* But Not the other three models, distributed through *Kost Kutter Stores* But Not the other outlets. By defining the boundaries between trouble and no trouble, he narrowed the problem from a general to a specific one and added a great deal to what he knew.

Now he could ask questions. What's wrong with the finish? It's scratched. What's different about Model A, compared to the other three? Model A costs less, weighs less, and is packed in a lighter carton. What's different about the way Kost Kutter handles our product, compared to other distributors who don't have any trouble? Kost Kutter uses local contract truckers instead of its own trucks, as the others do. With this information, the product manager could focus quickly on the way Kost Kutter handled Model A as an explanation.

If Model A remains undamaged at all the other distribution points, but gets scratched at Kost Kutter, there must be something different in the way Kost Kutter handles the product. Kost Kutter also handles the other three models the same way. But the Model A is packed in a lighter carton, so it slides around when it is transported by the local carriers and suffers damage, while the other models, in heavier cartons, don't.

You ask a But Not question for each of the What-Where-When questions. You confine yourself to what you actually observe. You ask, "What's wrong?" and then ask, "But what's not wrong? What's okay and not affected?" The finish is scratched, but the mechanism is fine. In this way you are trying to establish the limits of the deficiency. "Where are you not hearing complaints? How about the other distributors?" But Not questions tell you there is trouble only with the finish, only with Model A, only with Kost Kutter.

People aren't used to asking But Not questions. Why try to learn about where problems aren't occurring? When you show people how much clearer your picture of the problem becomes when you know where the boundary lies between the problem Is and the problem Is Not, and when they realize what you can find out when you ask what makes the difference, they see the point and begin to ask But Not questions of their own. But Not questions are sometimes difficult to put into words, and in some situations they don't make much sense. But you should always find out What, Where, and When there is Not an effect. There will always be positive information about What, Where, and When there is not a problem. It is as important to know the Not as it is to know the Is. It helps you answer Why?

The But Not question is an aid to collaboration. It enables you and your colleagues to see the limits of the problem. If you put the Is and the But Not information up on a board or easel pad where it is visible to everyone, the difference will jump out and help you find the cause of the problem.

Reach out beyond your own knowledge. Ask other people who are closer to the problem than you are about the differences between the Is and the Is Not. The crucial difference is often something that people close to the problem will recognize, whereas outsiders won't. The telephone, fax, e-mail, and group computing become invaluable in asking the Is and the But Not questions. You can extend your reach into local knowledge even from a distance. If you don't question the people who know, you'll never get the answer.

Finding the Facts of the Matter

Drawing an exact portrait of the problem is an exercise in rational thinking. You gather information to answer a series of specific questions. Speculation and intuition are neither needed nor allowed. You want the facts, as straight and as objectively stated as possible. You see it; you observe it; you report it. If you don't see it but still think it might be there, forget it for now. Your portrait of the problem must be as free of error and uncertainty as you can make it.

Experience and intuition will be useful later on when you search for an explanation. Then you will use everything you know to understand how this effect could have been created. But at this point you want the facts and nothing but the facts about the problem. You want to keep out anything that might confuse your perception of what is actually wrong.

It is hard to concentrate solely on the facts because we want to find out why something is occurring. Our explanation will be incomplete, however, if we base it on an inaccurate perception of the problem. We need discipline in the questions we ask and in the answers we accept. The expanded version of Kipling's six helpers tells you what to ask and creates a framework, shown in Figure 9-1, into which you enter the answers you get. When the framework is full, you will have drawn the best possible portrait

Figure 9–1. Framework for problem information.

	Problem IS . . .	But NOT . . .
Deficiency		
On What		
Who		
Where		
Where on the Object		
When		
When in the Sequence		
Unique Features		

of your problem. (The chart in Figure 9-1 can be distributed among the people in your working group.)

The framework contains a box for each kind of information. You have to have information about what the deficiency Is before you can understand the problem. The box reminds you of the question you must ask and the answer you must get. If the box is empty, you know your portrait of the problem is incomplete. The framework is a guide, a repository into which you put information, and a means of assessing the completeness of your picture of the problem.

The framework also leads you to the But Not questions you must ask. It helps you word the questions in ways that make sense, allows you to display the information you have so that you can see the boundaries and limits of the problem, and makes your information visible so you and your people can see gaps and errors to be corrected. Figure 9-1 can be put into a word processor in any computer as a form for gathering and organizing information. Simply keyboard in the information you gather to prepare a portrait of the problem you can fax or distribute to anyone who can use it.

HOW TO DO IT

You and your working group will gather information from your resource people through the questions you ask. You have a framework that tells you what the questions are and provides you with a place to put the answers when you get them. You may have to rephrase your questions and go to several sources to get the complete story. Your own judgment will tell you when you have enough and the right information. Use your own words in asking these questions, but be sure to cover everything set out in this guide.

1. *Set the task.*
   "What, in objective and specific terms, is our problem?"
   This tells your working group and your resource people what the task is so that you can draw a portrait of the problem in factual, specific words.

2. *Use the framework for questions and answers.*
   Before you've asked the question, you know what information you need. The framework guides and disciplines your information gathering. Organize the answers you get within the framework and make it visible on a board or chart pad so that everyone can see and have access to the information at the same time.

3. *Get out the Information, both Is and But Not.*
   Ask specific questions within each of the eight categories of the framework to focus your work group's thinking on the same aspect of the problem at the same time.
   "What's wrong? What's the deficiency?"
   "What object was the deficiency on?"
   "Where was the deficiency first seen?"
   "Where was the deficiency located on the object?"
   "When was the deficiency first seen?"
   "When in the sequence did the deficiency occur?"
   "What was unique or unusual or different about it?"
   "Who were the people involved?"
   Then you ask specific But Not questions to establish the limits and boundaries of the problem.
   "But what was Not affected? What's okay?"
   "But what other things were Not affected?"
   "But where was the deficiency Not seen?"
   "But where on the object was there Not an effect?"
   "But when was the deficiency Not seen?"
   "But when in the sequence did the deficiency Not occur?"
   "But who were the people Not affected or involved?"
   (Note that a Not question about Unique Features doesn't make sense.)

4. *Check for errors in the information.*
   Checking for errors is necessary and easy when the answers are written down and visible, but difficult when they are only presented verbally.
   "Is all of this information correct? Any errors?"
   Change the information and modify it until everyone agrees that it is correct and accurate.

5. *Check for gaps in the information.*
   Checking for gaps in the information is easy when the data are displayed in writing and almost impossible when they are presented verbally.

> **"Are we missing any information that we ought to have?"**
> An empty box in the framework or a partial answer tells you that
> something important is missing.
>
> 6. *Evaluate and agree on the problem.*
> **"Do we have a complete portrait of the problem now?"**
> Read the portrait out loud. Ask if anything is wrong or has been
> left out.
> **"Do we all agree that this is the problem we have to resolve?"**
> Make sure you all share an understanding of the problem and
> agree as to what it is.

Summary

Task 4 is to profile the problem by asking What, When, and
Where questions, displaying the answers within the problem
portrait framework, and leading your work group through these
steps:

1. Set the task.
2. Use the framework for questions and answers.
3. Get out the information, both Is and But Not.
4. Check for errors in the information.
5. Check for gaps in the information.
6. Evaluate and agree on the problem.

What caused the problem? How did it come into being?
Before you can resolve it in the most efficient way, you must
know why. That was Kipling's other question; determining its
answer is Task 5.

10

Task 5:
Knowing the Cause vs.
Simply Hoping You Are Right

Task 5 is knowing the cause of the problem instead of simply hoping that you are right about it. When you know why something has gone wrong, you are far better able to plan how to fix, correct, or improve it than if you are guessing or hoping.

The Problem with General Ideas

If you have only a general idea about what has caused a problem, you can take only general, broad actions if you want to be sure you have covered all the possibilities. Some of these actions may be ineffective, and others may cause new problems you didn't have before. But if you know exactly what caused the problem, you can take specific actions aimed at specific targets. These will always be more economical and efficient than general attempts to correct or improve a condition.

Yet many ordinary managers proceed on hope and a general idea rather than from certainty about causes. They say that it's not always possible to determine the real cause of a problem, so it's a waste of time to try to understand every specific one.

These managers pay a price for guessing instead of knowing, sometimes solving problems that don't exist and sometimes taking actions that don't solve anything. Knowing the cause leads you to a better choice of actions than depending upon guesswork. At least you know where you are and what is confronting you and can make sensible choices. People who manage beyond the ordinary determine the cause of a problem whenever possible.

Cause and Effect

It's almost always possible to determine the cause of a problem. Cause and effect are irrevocably linked. Consider the tracks a bear leaves in the snow. The bear is the cause; it leaves behind the exact impression of its foot, which is the effect to be explained. Old Trapper Dan studies the footprint in the snow and can tell how old the bear is, how big, whether it is male or female, how fast it was moving, and a surprising number of other things as well. The trapper draws on his experience and interprets the characteristics of the track in light of all he knows.

A manager and his colleagues study a problem—the effect of an undetermined and unknown cause—the same way. They draw on their experience and knowledge to interpret the characteristics of the problem, as described in the portrait they have made of it, in order to determine what kind of critter produced it. They know there is a one-to-one correspondence between the problem and its cause, just as there is between the foot and the track. If they know enough about the peculiarities of the problem and combine their knowledge and experience, they can usually recognize the exact cause.

But having a likely explanation doesn't guarantee that you have identified a precise cause. You can know that only when you have confirmed or proven that the likely explanation is in fact the cause. You confirm the cause when you have compared it against all the evidence you have gathered and see that it explains all of the details, without exception and without a lot of assumptions. You prove it when you conduct an independent experiment in which the cause produces exactly the effect you are trying to explain or when you find independent evidence that demonstrates the link of cause to effect.

PROVING THE CAUSE

Brownlee Engineering manufactures rocket bodies on subcontract to a prime contractor by wrapping carbon fiber around a polished steel mold in as many as twenty layers. Resin cements the filaments together. When it is dry, the wrapping is baked on the mold at high temperature for a long period of time, and then, when the mold has cooled, the carbon fiber shell is pulled off the mold and joined with other sections to form a finished rocket body.

Each rocket comprises three sections. Each section is eleven feet (3.35 meters) in diameter and seventeen feet (5.18 meters) long and is extremely strong and light. The sections go through quality inspection to make sure there are no voids or separations between the layers in the built-up section wall, as this would weaken the structure. For a number of months, the sections produced at Brownlee were within specifications. Then voids began to appear. This was a serious problem, since each section cost nearly $1 million when completed, and delivery delays to the prime contractor were not acceptable.

Examination of the defective sections showed that layers of carbon fiber were separating from the layers beneath them. These voids were occurring at different locations within the built-up section wall, and no clear relationship between the failure and manufacturing methods could be demonstrated. A number of possible causes and remedial actions were suggested.

The proposed actions were expensive and not very specific; they included increasing the amount of resin used to bind the carbon fiber, experimenting with shorter baking times, and redesigning the wrapping machine to control more closely tension on the carbon fiber. All the proposals would have required changes in the specifications and equipment, cost a lot of money, and caused more delivery delays. In desperation, Brownlee Engineering increased the rate of production to the maximum, hoping that enough good sections would be turned out to meet the schedule, reconciling themselves to absorbing the extra costs in overtime and waste.

Herb Hammond, the project manager, rejected these actions. He wanted to know *why* the problem was occurring. He therefore questioned people who were close to the project and pulled together information from all levels of the operation, and, in doing so, he uncovered some facts not previously considered. The rockets produced during the first six months had been without voids, and yet the amount of resin used, baking time, and tensions on the wrapping machine remained unchanged since then. So what was causing the problem?

Hammond identified some factors that had changed. The prime contractor had required that a new procedure be followed in preparing the mold. Before the carbon fiber was wrapped around it, the mold was treated with a slipcoat of Teflon® particles suspended in a lacquer carrier. This made it easier to pull the finished section off the mold when baking had been completed. The new procedure required that the dried slipcoat be buffed to a high gloss before the resin and the carbon fiber were applied.

In addition, a supervisor told Hammond that the size of the Teflon particles in the carrier had been increased at about the same time to enhance its lubrication effect. When asked about the slipcoat, an operator commented, "It used to be milky when you put it on, but now it isn't." He found that the larger, heavier Teflon particles settled out within a few minutes, leaving a slipcoat on the mold that was mainly dried lacquer, no longer "milky" from the suspended bits of lubricant. Much of this slipcoat was being buffed off, on orders from the prime contractor, to produce a high gloss. Hammond and his colleagues concluded that there simply wasn't enough Teflon left on the mold to act as an efficient lubricant. Because of the increased friction, it was necessary to pull harder to release the finished section, tearing apart the layers of carbon fiber.

But how could Hammond be sure? He and his co-workers checked the cause against the evidence and determined that insufficient slipcoat would explain all aspects of the problem. They confirmed the cause as consistent with the failure without making additional assumptions. They seemed to have a complete explanation.

But Hammond wanted to go further. He sought to prove his case. Information from the shop log showed that extraction pressures (the pull necessary to drag the section off the mold) had increased as much as 40 percent since the changes had been made. This demonstrated a one-to-one correspondence of cause to effect. In addition, a laboratory experiment that simulated extraction of the section from the mold under conditions both of heavy slipcoat and no buffing and of thin slipcoat with buffing produced a separation between layers in the latter state. More proof. Then a physical examination of a buffed mold showed that there was virtually no Teflon left on it to make extraction easier. Hammond considered the cause to be proved beyond reasonable doubt.

Change and Difference

Hammond and his people looked for change in their analysis of the rocket body separations. Production had been okay, then it began to have problems. Something must have changed. If none of the conditions of production had changed, quality would still be okay. So look for what was now different. They found changes in the buffing procedure and in the Teflon particle sizes. These produced an effect: less Teflon left on the mold. This in turn produced another change, the need to pull harder to remove the carbon shell from the mold. It was this extra pull that produced the tearing in the layers of carbon fiber.

When a problem appears, look for change. The change may have occurred immediately before appearance of the problem, or it may have occurred a long time ago. The negative effects of change can take quite a while to become evident, making the link between the change and the effect harder to find, but the logic is the same. Change may be fast or slow, but a deterioration in performance indicates that some change, somewhere, at some time, has taken place.

The contrast between what the problem Is observed to be, and the But Not is where you look for clues to change. If the trouble was first observed on June 1 in District 7 but not in other districts, look for a change that occurred before June in District 7 but not in the others, and ignore any changes that came after June 1. It's so simple that it hardly seems worth saying, but many managers don't understand how to find the critical change. They look everywhere, even where the relevant change couldn't have occurred.

If the problem has been around for a long time, look for differences and unique factors. One model of household thermostat gave erratic readings after installation, while other models made by the same company did not. The thermostat performed well in the laboratory, but customers complained that it made the furnace run all the time in cold weather, once it was installed on the wall. What was different? The erratic model was the cheapest of the line, and material costs had been cut to the bone. The insulating pad at the back of the thermostat, which kept the cold wall from distorting the thermostat's reading of the room's air temperature, was of lower insulating value than the pad used in the other models. When placed on a wall that was cooled by outside air, the thermostat recorded how cold the wall was, not how warm the air was inside the room, and kept the furnace working overtime.

When you know the cause, you can often find an easy way to correct the problem. The case of the problems with Brown-lee's rocket bodies clearly illustrates this. Production engineers suggested a complicated continuous mixing machine, a more complex way of applying the slipcoat, and an automated control procedure that would measure the thickness of the polished slipcoat before wrapping. These would have resolved the prob-lem, but would have cost a lot of time and money and required extra personnel. One operator then suggested to Hammond, "Right now we have trouble because we can't tell how much Teflon is on the mold. Why not color the Teflon blue so we can see how much is in the mixture, how much we're putting on, and how much is left on after buffing?" The Teflon was colored bright blue, and the operators were given instructions how to use it. This resolved the problem quickly and at practically no cost. When people who know a lot about a problem understand the cause, they often come up with simple, excellent resolutions.

To solve the problem with the rockets, Hammond probed and dug for the information he got. He asked, "Why? Why do you think that? Tell me more." He used his people well. He let them know that he thought their knowledge and ideas were worthwhile. As a result, they told him everything they knew and thought about the problem, including the simple idea of color-ing the Teflon. And he *listened* to what they said. He helped them put their ideas together and drew out the fragments of informa-tion that made sense when put together. The comment from an operator that the slipcoat "used to be milky but isn't now" might easily have been missed, but he caught it. More than any other piece of information, this led to the resolution of a multi-million-dollar problem.

Hammond wasn't a genius who knew all the answers; he simply was a manager who asked questions of the people who knew things he didn't. He talked to them in the shop and over the telephone. He used fax and e-mail to get information from people outside his immediate reach. He didn't hold any big meetings. But he did pull together more and better information than anyone else had. He drew out theories of cause from the people close to the trouble, then proved the cause beyond doubt. With the collaboration of his people, he did a more thorough analysis of the problem, went beyond the ordinary, and resolved the problem at very low cost.

Using All Modes of Thinking

It doesn't make much difference where the explanation of a problem comes from, as long as it can be confirmed and proven. All modes of thinking are useful and appropriate. A winning idea is a winning idea regardless of where it comes from.

Intuition and experience provide most ideas about cause because there are few things new under the sun. Those of us who have amassed years of experience on the job know tens of thousands of causes for tens of thousands of problems. Another manager, confronted with voids in the rocket bodies and drawing upon a different background of experience, might have said, "It sounds to me like they're pulling too hard and the layers are torn apart when they draw the shell off." And he might have proceeded from that suspected cause to find out and demonstrate why, uncovering other information along the way. Or he might have started from a dozen other initial observations and asked why, why, why, until he uncovered the real cause.

An idea about causation can come from anyone, from anywhere, and can be inspired by anything. What is important is that it be *confirmed*, that it be consistent with all that is known about the effect, that it explain everything and make logical good sense, and that it be provable through independent experiment. It is legitimate for someone to say, "I already know why" on the basis of past experience, knowledge, hunch, guess, or gut feeling. But it is wrong, dangerous, and sometimes suicidal to take action without confirming or proving that the intuition is correct. Any explanation, from any source, is speculation until confirmed or proved.

To confirm or prove an idea about cause is to subject a statement of cause-and-effect to rational thinking before it can be accepted. No matter what the source of the idea, it must account for *all* the details of the problem that were actually observed, and it must make good sense. No matter what the idea, it must survive an empirical, independent experiment in which the supposed cause produces an effect identical to that observed as the problem.

All theories of cause must meet the requirements of rational thinking, regardless of the mode of thinking from which they originated. This is the control that allows us to use ideas from experience, hunch, and imagination in the resolution of problems. An idea can come from anywhere. These are then put into a statement of cause-and-effect that can be logically tested. If a cause statement is confirmed or proven, the explanation is as legitimate and solid as any can be. But it must progress from hunch to a declarative statement, "This caused that," which must then stand up to logic and make practical sense if it is to be acceptable.

Ordinary managers often do not understand this point. They overlook their own subordinates as suppliers of vital information from which to suggest, confirm, or prove explanations. They don't trust intuitive and experiential thinking; they think it is speculation and fantasy and cannot be relied upon. That is wrong. Anyone can come up with the right cause, from any source of inspiration or past memory. Anyone can be the source of a million-dollar explanation. What is absolutely essential is to put the idea into a logical statement and to prove it, to convert speculation to legitimate, objective information.

"But I don't need to know what caused it," some managers say. That may be true if the cause is obvious and makes sense, you know what the problem is, and the need for action is imperative. Or you may not care what the cause is if you're dealing with a one-time thing or an accident. Maybe you can determine later what caused it. Maybe finding an explanation is someone else's responsibility and your job is simply to develop a way of dealing with the situation at hand. If you really don't need to know what caused a problem, you don't need to bother with it and can go on to actions to resolve the situation.

There is another case where you don't need to know the cause of the problem, and that is when you decide to proceed by another route entirely. You may choose to avoid the problem by reengineering the situation so that the problem can no longer occur. For example, there might be competition and conflict over use of scarce computer facilities in your office. Dealing with the cause might entail setting priorities, placing limitations on use time, and a lot of other steps. You might instead choose to manage around the problem and avoid the whole issue by purchasing a number of PCs to take care of the overload. Buying more computing power eliminates the problem. Managing around the problem is another case of restating the purpose, as considered in Task 2. It may be the most efficient way of dealing with the problem in many instances. Always consider managing around the problem as another way to resolve difficulties and improve the operation.

But be warned: It is easy to convince yourself that a step in any discipline can be skipped: "I don't need to bother with proving the cause because everybody knows what brings on this kind of trouble." Assuming that the cause would be proved if you only took the time to do it is suicidal. Saying, "We haven't time for a lot of questions right now" is stupid and dangerous. Shortcuts of this nature can take you to managing at the lowest level of the ordinary. Take time to think: "Can I really take action without knowing what caused this? If I don't know, will I be able to produce a good enough set of actions to resolve it?" If you have any doubt whatsoever, take the time to ask why and prove your case.

Knowing why something happened and being able to prove it is essential if you hope to prevent the same thing from happening again or if you ever expect improvement. Knowing why is a vital part of managing beyond the ordinary. If you don't know why, you are in the dark. If you do know why and know that you are correct in your explanation, you will be able to see how to make things better in the most direct manner possible. Going beyond the ordinary, in most cases, depends on knowing why and being able to prove it.

HOW TO DO IT

First you ask, "Do we know what the cause is?" If you can answer yes and prove it, go on to the next task. If you have any doubt, stop now and dig a little deeper. You and your working group will ask questions to find an explanation. Why? Why? Ask why over and over of your resource people. From their firsthand knowledge they can tell you things you wouldn't otherwise know. You and your work group will need to follow these steps:

1. *Set the task.*
   "Why did it happen? What caused this problem? And how can we prove it?"
   This tells your colleagues that the task is to both explain and prove the explanation. It encourages them to be both imaginative and disciplined in their thinking.

2. *Review the problem.*
   "This is what we have to explain, both the observed Is and the But Not sides of the problem."
   Refer back to your portrait of the problem in its visible framework as you developed it in Task 4. This will review the content of the problem and provide a focus for the creative work to follow.

3. *Search for changes.*
   "What changes have taken place that could have caused or had any effect on this problem?"
   Focus your group on known or suspected changes and follow up on any clues or comments in this direction.
   "Have any improvements, modifications, substitutions, or alterations been made?"
   "What did you mean by that? Tell me more."
   Dig out any information about change. Write down comments about changes, and make them visible to everyone. List the changes so that you can refer back to them as you begin to make testable cause-and-effect statements.

4. *Explore differences.*
   "What's different about the problem Is, compared to the But Not?"
   Explore all the differences you can find, particularly in the Defi-

ciency, Where, and When. Follow up on any comments that might lead to a difference, irregularity, or anomaly.

"Could you explain that?"
Dig out any information about differences. Record comments about differences, and make them visible to everyone. List the differences so that you can refer back to them as you make testable cause-and-effect statements.

5. *Explore unique features.*
"What's unique, unusual, surprising, unexpected, or curious about any of this? What catches your attention?"
Explore any unique features or unusual events or conditions that you observe, and ask why they catch your eye.

"Why does this seem unique or unusual? What does it mean?"
Follow up anything unique or unusual to see if it points to a change or difference that could lead to the cause. What is unique about it? List unique features so that you can refer back to them as you make testable cause-and-effect statements.

6. *Formulate testable statements of cause.*
"What cause-and-effect statements about the problem can we make from this?"
Make a declarative statement for each possible cause—"These factors and conditions caused that effect"—that can then be tested to produce either "Yes, it did" or "No, it didn't" as a clear conclusion.

"Can this statement be logically tested?"
Be sure it will yield a clear yes or no answer.

"Can we make any other statements about cause?"
Get as many reasonable statements of cause as you can. Make them visible, and save them for confirmation and proof steps.

7. *Confirm the cause.*
"Does this cause account for all the effects observed in the original problem?"
Review the effects listed in the portrait of the problem, and for each one, ask, "Does this cause account for this effect? Would this cause logically produce this result?"

"Do any assumptions have to be made to enable this cause to account for these effects?"
Follow up and verify whether the assumptions are supported in fact.

"Do we agree that this evidence confirms this cause as true?"

Get positive agreement that the cause has been confirmed beyond a reasonable doubt.

8. *Prove the cause.*
**"What independent experiment can we conduct to show that
this produced that effect?"**
Design an experiment that will replicate the cause-and-effect
sequence and provide an unequivocal yes or no answer.
Conduct the experiment and examine the results.
If the causal conditions produce the predicted effects, accept
the cause-and-effect statement as proven. If they fail to produce
the predicted effects, examine the experiment to see that it
makes logical sense, and correct and repeat if necessary. If it is
logically sound and doesn't produce the expected effects, consider the cause unproven, and look for another explanation.
**"Do we agree that this experiment has proven the cause to be
true?"**
Get positive agreement on the interpretation of results.
**"What additional independent evidence can we present to
prove that this caused that?"**
Identify any new evidence that can be presented as a natural
experiment to prove a cause-and-effect statement. Make sure it
will provide an unequivocal yes or no answer.
**"Complete a cause-and-effect statement using the new evi-
dence, test it logically, and examine the results.**
As earlier, if the causal conditions produce the predicted effects,
accept the cause-and-effect statement as proven; if they fail, reject it.
**"Do we agree that this new evidence has proved the cause to
be true?"**
Get positive agreement on the interpretation of results.

9. *Summarize your conclusions about the cause.*
Make a summary statement concerning your findings about the
cause. Make it visible so that everyone can see and comment
on it.
**"Do we agree that this is an accurate statement of what has
caused the problem we want to resolve?"**

Summary

Task 5 is to determine and prove the cause. An explanation can
come from any source, but it must be confirmed and proved

before it can be accepted as true. You do this by asking Why over and over and then subjecting the answers you get to stringent rational, logical inspection. You lead your colleagues through the task of finding the cause by the questions you ask and by taking these steps:

1. Set the task.
2. Review the problem.
3. Search for changes.
4. Explore differences.
5. Explore unique features.
6. Formulate testable statements of cause.
7. Confirm the cause.
8. Prove the cause.
9. Summarize your conclusions about the cause.

Now that you have proved the cause, what to do about it? Determining what needs to be fixed, corrected, improved, or avoided by whatever actions you may take, is the goal of Task 6.

11

Task 6: Setting the Requirements for Improvement vs. Jumping Directly to Alternatives

At this point you are ready to take action to resolve a problem, but what is that action supposed to do? You can't build a good house unless the plans for it are worked out before you begin. The same applies to building a complete resolution for a complex problem. Knowing what you need to repair, improve, correct, or avoid in the problem situation and making these your requirements for action is Task 6 if you are going to manage beyond the ordinary.

"Look before you leap," as folk wisdom puts it, is an essential part of managing beyond the ordinary. Look and think first; then act. You have limited amounts of time, money, and effort, and you need to make them all count. If you are going to do more than ordinarily well at management, you have to be sure those resources are put where they will accomplish the most good. You can't afford to waste anything, and that takes careful thinking about what you need to do before you start to do it.

Dealing With All the Issues

In any complex problem, a number of actions will be required and a number of issues will have to be dealt with to resolve whatever has gone wrong. You want to set things right again. But to do that, you have to fix, improve, correct, or avoid *all* the important issues that accompany the problem or were caused by it, in addition to the main problem. Unless you think through what all those issues are, you will overlook some and produce an incomplete resolution.

Suppose you provide an accounting service to small businesses. Your clients depend on you to keep their records straight and legal. Now you find out that one of your visiting accountants has misunderstood or been unaware of a certain tax provision and has significantly understated your clients' obligations to the government. The problem and its cause are clear. Your clients have discovered that they owe a lot more in taxes than they expected to because your employee failed to set aside enough money. They are furious that they are in trouble with the government because one of your workers didn't know or do what he should have.

Is the problem only that your employee made a mistake and now should be disciplined and trained in the proper procedures? Not on your life! It's a lot wider than that. There are issues arising out of the problem that are as important as the problem itself. Your clients are angry, and some are talking of going to a competitor. You have a legal liability of unknown size. Your reputation is threatened. Other clients are in a panic and asking if their accounts can be trusted. The phone is ringing off the hook, and all the news is bad. And on and on, like waves generated by a large rock dropped into a quiet pool.

All these issues have to be recognized, thought through, and acted on for the problem situation to be resolved properly. You can't just call your employee on the carpet and chew him out. That would be managing in the ordinary way. Instead, you need to be aware of all the issues so that you can know what's important and has to be handled right now. You have to face each issue and deal with it before you can say the problem has been resolved. You have to inventory all the issues so that you don't miss any. Your list of issues becomes your table of requirements for a complete resolution.

Many managers go directly from "We know the problem and the cause" to "Let's do something about it." They don't take a moment to think, "What do we need to repair, improve, correct, or avoid in this situation?" So they overlook important items and don't fully resolve the problem, dealing with it piecemeal instead. And the parts that haven't been handled cause other problems, and the problem gets bigger rather than smaller.

When you manage beyond the ordinary, you recognize the problem, find its cause, and then ask, "What should we do about it?" First, you must define the "it." How do you find out what all the issues are? Ask the people who know firsthand about the problem. They'll tell you what needs to be done. And don't be surprised if they tell you about issues you didn't know were involved. They know what the issues are because they know what the problem's side effects have been. They know about the little things that cause pain and disruption, and they know from experience that these are often overlooked as unimportant. They can tell you what happens when these smaller issues are skipped over because they are the ones who end up working harder to make a bad plan survive, and they don't want that to happen again.

The Ideal Resolution

What are you trying to achieve when you resolve a problem? You hope to achieve an ideal, complete resolution, or as close to it as you can get. You don't want to aim for the bare minimum or a halfway resolution. So you stretch your mind and imagine the perfect resolution, the best that can possibly be, the ideal. If you reach for the stars, there is no guarantee you will get there. But if you don't reach for them, you are assured you won't come close.

"These are the things that would have to be done to achieve a perfect resolution," you and your colleagues say. You make inputs from your collective knowledge and experience. Then you list the things you consider essential, and these make up your specifications for an ideal resolution. If you can achieve them all, you have achieved perfection. If you can accomplish only 90 percent of them, you know you have reached 90 percent of the ideal, and that isn't bad. But if you don't identify which elements make up a perfect resolution and don't state them as requirements and set their completion as a goal, you won't know how well you have done or what else you might have achieved if you had thought about it a little more at the time.

When you specify the characteristics of an ideal resolution, you can choose specific actions to fit each specific issue from your experience, knowledge, intuition, and imagination. This allows you to build up the most efficient program of actions to resolve the problem situation as a whole. You define perfection, then come as close to it as you can.

Types of Action

In dealing with any problem, four types of action are open to you. Thinking about all four provides a focus for your colleagues as they identify what needs to be done. When you look at a problem situation, you can say:

1. "It's broken, so let's *repair* it."
2. "It could perform better, so let's *improve* it."
3. "It's doing the wrong thing, so let's *correct* it."
4. "It may do the wrong thing in the future, so let's do something now to *avoid* or *prevent* it."

Repairing

Repairing something is the most immediate action. It implies returning something to the utility it had before the trouble appeared: "The gizmo arm is broken, so let's repair it." But getting the item back into shape is the end to achieve, nothing more. You don't make it any better but only try to make it as good as it was. Repairing the arm may call for welding, replacing, making a new one, bolting together a substitute, or any one of a thousand fixes that knowledge of the craft suggests. When you ask, "What has to be repaired in this situation?" people will look for immediate actions to reinstate something to its previous level of usefulness.

Improving

Improving something is looking beyond the immediate: "The gizmo arm is broken again, so let's make it stronger." You want to get it back in shape, but you also want it better and more durable. Improving it may call for strengthening it, making it of tougher materials, modifying it, or any one of many actions that will restore its operation at a higher plane of quality and reliability. When you ask, "How can we improve this situation?" people will look beyond the immediate fix to see what they can do to make fixes less frequent by making things better.

Correcting

Correcting something is looking still further beyond the immediate. It is looking at the item's purpose and evaluating how well it is performing at present: "This gizmo arm was built wrong in the first place, so let's redesign it so it won't break." Correcting something is finding and understanding the cause of the problem, then doing something to modify the cause so it can no longer act to create that problem: "Vibration causes the metal of the arm to crystallize and weaken. If we redesign the arm to withstand vibration, it should last a lot longer."

In making a correction, you are taking a new and different direction, doing something in a different way so that the effect of the cause is reduced or eliminated. When you ask, "How can we correct this situation?" people will think creatively about cause and effect and start from the premise that the old way is not good enough.

Avoiding

Avoiding trouble is finding a way to keep the problem from happening altogether. This thinking is the furthest from the immediate: "The gizmo arm is always breaking. Let's redesign the machine so it doesn't need a gizmo arm, or let's install rubber mounts to absorb the vibration." Avoiding trouble is finding a way around the situation so that the cause is removed or neutralized. This requires full knowledge of the cause and the circumstances that enable it to create the problem you want to get rid of, and this in turn requires looking for another, different way of doing things.

To avoid something, focus on the cause and go over or under or around it in such a way that it no longer gives you trouble. When you ask, "How can we avoid this problem?" people will think about how to remove or neutralize or get around the cause.

Which Action to Choose?

You can choose to look at any situation in the immediate present, in the near time frame, or far out into the future. The action you choose depends on how far ahead you focus your attention. The further ahead you look, the more options are open to you. To manage beyond the ordinary, you always want to look as far ahead as you can.

Going for the Ideal Resolution

The Stanworth Glass Company had a high-pressure air compressor on its bottle line that was critical to production. The compressor broke down from time to time whenever a hose assembly blew out. Replacement never took more than fifteen minutes, but it threw production off. The maintenance people knew the part number by heart, 2BF37, and would trot to the supply department. Supply always had extras on hand because they were needed so often. When the hose was replaced, production could start up again—until the next time. It wasn't a big problem, but it was inconvenient and frustrating.

The foreman, Bert Wallace, got tired of the routine. He went to one of his maintenance people and asked, "How could we avoid this problem?" The maintenance person answered, "Easy. Get a hose that won't blow out."

So they looked beyond simple replacement to find a blowout-proof hose. They consulted the specs and found the hose that should be used was a 2BF41, a special high-pressure hose, not a low-pressure 2BF37. The wrong hose had gotten on the compressor and had been replaced and replaced by force of habit. They put on a 41—and no more blowouts. Simple. Yet if Wallace and his maintenance person hadn't thought beyond the obvious replacement of the hose, they'd still be waiting for the next blowout!

It is necessary to think of the perfect resolution, then name the things that need to be done to achieve it to find the actions that will produce the ideal. Ordinary managers don't think of the ideal because they feel perfection is unobtainable and not practical. But how do you know it is unobtainable if you don't try? If you imagine the ideal, you may find there is a resolution that achieves it, or at least comes close. Remember the case of the rocket bodies in the previous chapter? The operator said to himself, "What would be an ideal way to prevent having too little Teflon on the mold? Color it blue so you could at least see it!" And a resolution became available that saved millions of dollars. Resolutions like that are out there, and you can find them if you look. If you look and don't find one, you haven't lost much. If you don't look, you will never know what you may have passed up.

All four types of action are legitimate and good in their place. Just repairing something is often the right thing to do. But if you look further and find something nobody else ever saw before, you've discovered a resolution that will pay off for a long time to come. We believe that looking ahead, whether to define criteria or requirements for action or to anticipate what might go wrong in a future situation, is a mark of superior intelligence. That ability was a key to human survival in more perilous times. The person who could anticipate the tiger lived longer than the one who couldn't. The manager who can visualize an ideal resolution will select better courses of action than the one who does not and may be around longer as a result.

Stimulating Innovation Through Collaboration

Most people need to be stimulated to become innovative, and they need to be helped to find creative, new answers in their funds of knowledge and memory, instead of coming up with the same old answers. The new answers are there, but it's sometimes difficult to get at them.

You can elicit these nuggets of inspiration by stating the specifications of the ideal resolution for a problem as a first step. Your colleagues can then search their brains for ideas to meet each individual specification. The specification gives them the address in their memory banks so that they can find the stored-away facts they need. One person may have the whole answer, as the operator in the rocket bodies example did. Or a person may have only a partial answer, a glimmer of a resolution, and that partial answer will inspire another person to pull out another idea that builds on the preceding one. Then another idea will be triggered by that one. Creative thinking is cumulative and flourishes when properly stimulated.

All of us know more than we think we do and have information stored away of which we aren't consciously aware. We need time to get it out, and we need encouragement to dig into that stack of knowledge, some of which we may think is trivial and unimportant. We need to know that it's all right to bring out a new, perhaps even a far-out idea. We've been trained over the years to tell ourselves, "No, that wouldn't work, and people might think it's just plain nutty" and to keep all but the safest ideas to ourselves. Yet the best requirements for a resolution are the ones that stretch the imagination to create something new and decidedly better than what has gone before. Intuitive and creative thinking depend on the assurance that it's all right to imagine and speculate. Let your colleagues know that you welcome all kinds of ideas.

Collaboration says, "Let's build something together that none of us could create alone." By thinking together, you and your co-workers assemble a complete answer that has never been stated before and that meets or comes close to the ideal. Yet none of you could have done it without help. Each person needed the stimulation of other people's ideas to draw out the gold that was hidden in memory. One good idea makes another possible.

PLANNING FOR ACTION

The technical staff of one of the largest international banking institutions in the world had just created a complex procedure for exchanging financial information securely between branches in microseconds. A conference was to be held at which banking officials from more than one hundred nations would receive instruction in how to use the new procedure.

Such conferences had been held in the past, and there had always been confusion and considerable argument at them. The new procedures had never worked as well as expected because they hadn't been fully understood and correctly implemented. It usually took months for a new procedure to be debugged and operate at an acceptable level. Many officials felt that the organization was too diverse for there to be universal acceptance of anything.

Ruth Ingersoll was informed that she would organize and lead the conference. She felt that this assignment took her beyond what she knew, so she selected three others to form a working group with her. The group found that past conferences had followed a standard format, regardless of the content, each one copying the pattern followed by the one before. The group felt that there should be a better way of designing a conference.

The four officers consulted a number of people to determine what the attending officials would have to learn in order to explain the new procedure to their own staffs and make it work. They also found out what these officials already knew that could be built upon and what they didn't know that they would have to be supplied with. In addition, they found out what other procedures would interface with the new one and identified points of conflict and possible confusion.

To do this in a worldwide organization in an ordinary way might have taken weeks or months. But it didn't take the group long in spite of the distances involved. The four officers used the telephone, fax machine, e-mail, and team computing where available and got the best thinking of dozens of people about what was needed for a successful introduction of the new procedure. People collaborated across thousands of miles of sea and land, people who had never met each other or worked together before, brought together through modern technology so that they could combine their ideas as readily as if they were seated together around a table.

The four officers created a list of requirements for an ideal presentation, one that would address each of the essential issues in turn. These became the design criteria for the conference. With this list of requirements, it was easy for Ingersoll and her working group to assemble the best ideas for dealing with each issue. They then put the very best ideas together to form a plan for the conference.

When the day came, the presentation went off flawlessly. Everything presented was relevant. Major problems were identified, and ways around them were described. Nothing was left out, and nothing was put in that didn't have a purpose. The attending officials were enthusiastic, since they were not being talked down to or overwhelmed with details they didn't need. The new procedure was up and running within days, and there were no unfortunate surprises. Ingersoll and her group received compliments for planning "the best conference this institution has ever held."

Decide what you need to do, then do it. That's what Ruth Ingersoll and her work group did. It sounds easy, and it is. But doing what needs to be done becomes almost impossible if you don't first establish, clearly and explicitly, what needs doing. Ask yourself the critical question: "What do we need to repair, improve, correct, or avoid?" Then you can go ahead with a clear prescription for what constitutes an ideal resolution. Your set of requirements becomes your blueprint for the resolution you will build.

HOW TO DO IT

Ask your resource people, "What has to be repaired, improved, corrected, or avoided to resolve this problem and its associated issues?" Use all the communication media available to you: phone, fax, e-mail, team computing, casual conversation, and formal meeting to gather ideas. You and your working group will form your criteria for the ideal resolution from the suggestions you gather by taking these steps:

1. *Set the task.*
   "What do we need to repair, improve, correct, or avoid in this situation?"
   This tells your working group that the task is to state what is to be accomplished by this resolution and focuses attention on the types of action that are required.

2. *Review the problem, the issues, and the cause.*
   "This is what we have to resolve."

State the problem, the issues, and the cause you and your group have found. Refer back to your portrait of the problem and its issues and to the cause you have proven. This will review the situation and focus on what is relevant.

"Are we all agreed on this?"

Make sure that everyone has a shared understanding of the problem, issues, and cause. Clear up any confusion before moving on.

3. *Identify the things that need to be repaired.*

   "What do we need to repair or fix up?"

   Focus first on what is wrong that needs to be repaired to make things right. Your resource people will want to talk about concrete repair actions and fixes. Lead the discussion back to the things and issues that need repair.

   "We'll talk about how to fix them later, but now we want to say just what needs repair."

   You might also ask them what they would be repairing by the specific actions they suggest.

4. *Question whether repair is good enough.*

   "Is repairing it good enough? Can we improve or correct it, instead?"

   Shift focus from immediate repair to longer-range actions. Show that repair actions will last only for a short time and ask if protection over a longer period is possible.

   "Can we improve it or make it better so that we won't have to fix it again?"

   Elicit ideas for improvement, and list them. Give your co-workers time to build and expand their ideas.

   "Can we correct or redesign it so that we won't have to repair it again?"

   Elicit ideas for correction or redesign, and list them. Give people time to think, imagine, and organize their thoughts.

5. *Question whether avoiding the problem is possible.*

   "What can we do to avoid this problem altogether?"

   Get out ideas about how to avoid or get around the problem. Give your resource people time to think and develop their ideas.

   "Can you tell me more about that?"

   Draw people out, and encourage them to put their ideas into words and concrete proposals. Don't rush them. Finding workable avoidance actions doesn't come easily.

6. *Always ask for another round.*
   "Is there anything else we need to repair, improve, correct, or avoid?"
   The simplest, most effective ideas often come out last and can be cut off if the resource person is rushed. One suggestion can trigger another and lead to a synthesis of ideas that goes beyond the original ones if people have time to think and discuss.

7. *Agree on what needs to be done.*
   "Are we agreed that we need to act on each of these things?"
   Get positive agreement that these are the things that need to be done to produce the ideal resolution.
   "Are we agreed that these will be our criteria for creating our best possible resolution?"
   Make sure people understand that the things they have listed to be repaired, improved, corrected, or avoided will be used as the design specifications for the actions they will choose to resolve the problem.
   "Then this will be the blueprint we will follow in creating our resolution."

Summary

Task 6 is to determine what actions need to be taken to resolve the problem and its associated issues completely. You can identify these actions by asking what the ideal and perfect resolution would be and taking that as your set of criteria for creating the best possible practical resolution. You lead your people through this task by the questions you ask and by following these steps:

1. Set the task.
2. Review the problem, the issues, and the cause.
3. Identify the things that need to be repaired.
4. Question whether repair is good enough.
5. Question whether avoiding the problem is possible.

6. Always ask for another round.
7. Agree on what needs to be done.

But what are you actually going to do? Pulling together your co-workers' best knowledge and ideas about which actions will satisfy your criteria is Task 7.

12

Task 7:
Finding the Best Possible
Actions vs. Accepting
the First That Come Along

We are finally at the point of action. We're about to build our resolution, and we want to make it as good as we can. Task 7 is to assemble an inventory of the best ideas available for making things better. Why an inventory? You want to create a pool of the best ideas possible so that you can pick out the very best to use in building your resolution. If you draw from the best of the best available, you will create the best resolution possible given the present circumstances and knowledge.

The logic of this task is purely common sense. If you have only a few ideas about the problem, drawn from people who don't know much about it, you won't have much to work with. But if you gather all the best ideas from the very best informed people, those who know the problem firsthand and have thought about it a lot, you will have a great deal more to work with, in both quality and quantity. You are far more likely to find the ultimate good answer if you have a large, high quality pool of ideas to draw from.

The ordinary way of managing is to pull together the first set of suggestions that provides a credible course of action. This is doing no more than is necessary. The manager who works this way takes the first ideas that sound all right and cobbles them together into a rough plan. The ordinary way says that further adjustments and refinements—if they are needed, which they probably won't be because this is a great idea with nothing at all wrong with it and an outstanding plan as it is—can be added after the actions have been taken. Most of the time and effort with this approach are put in after the decisions are made and are spent on getting a lousy plan to work, redoing large parts of it, tweaking and shoring up its weak points.

Contrast this management style to the way you would do it if you truly wanted to go beyond the ordinary. You would study your blueprint, your list of requirements, which tells you exactly what you need to get done. Then you would spend most of your effort getting the best inputs and ideas for your resolution, finding the highest quality ideas and information available. You would ask the best-informed people you could find for their best thinking. You would put their ideas together in a reservoir of knowledge, from which you could cull the very best to be used in drafting your resolution. Thought and effort spent at the front end of the action selection process pays off.

Don't settle for the first ideas put forward. The simple, most efficient ideas about anything usually evolve after a little time and considerable thinking have been invested. These ideas are often combinations and outgrowths of earlier ideas; one formulation, discussed and thoughtfully considered, often leads to another that is even more efficient and easier to implement and that does more for you at less cost.

There are two ways of arriving at the best resolution. The first is called a *design* decision and calls for putting together different actions to meet each of your criteria, selecting components from your pool of possibilities and designing your resolution from scratch. The second is called a *choice* decision because you choose between existing, ready-made alternatives (e.g., different types of computers, sites for the new office, or people to fill a position). In this case, your task is to create a pool of alternative choices and find the best package of elements to satisfy all of your criteria at one time. You don't need to build the ideal resolution from scratch because your alternatives are ready-made, off-the-shelf entities.

Seeking New Ways to Reach a Resolution

There is almost always more than one way to do something: "the right way, the wrong way, and our organization's way," as some uncharitable persons put it. Organizations become fixed on particular ways of doing things and frozen into habitual ways of acting. Searching for the best way to do something, among a collection of people who are well-informed about it, is the most effective way of getting out of the rut. People have ideas because they can't help it. They see a problem situation, think about it, and wonder how it could be improved. If you ask them, "What do you think about this?" they'll tell you. They may have had these good ideas for a while, but no one has ever asked their opinion. Now you are asking them, and they are eager to share what they know. Since they know the situation firsthand, they can give you practical suggestions on how their ideas can be implemented and what is necessary to make them succeed.

Always remember that there is usually more than one way to reach a resolution. Ask your colleagues if they can't think of another approach to consider. If a new direction appears, ask questions to expand on it. Get people to describe the new way in detail. Don't let someone else cut off the exploration of a new way just because it is different. Find out all your resource people have in mind.

You want only relevant and useful ideas, not anything and everything that pops into people's minds. You are not asking people to brainstorm the question in an uncontrolled fashion, spewing out anything that occurs to them. You are seeking the best ideas about the problem in a highly focused manner. You have listed your criteria, the things that will have to be accomplished in order to make the resolution complete. Now you are asking the people who know to tell you what their thoughts are with respect to each of those specific things.

FINDING THE BEST WAY

Juan Ortega was a manager for Western Grains, a large commodities trading company. He had been directed to establish a new grain buying and shipping station in Kansas that would have the latest in grain storage, cleaning, and drying facilities and could also offer a selection of farming equipment and supplies if that would be useful in building the business. The problem now was to determine where the station should be located and what services it should offer.

Ortega felt that he needed the ideas of experienced people, so he assembled a group of colleagues who knew a lot about the area and the needs of the farm population. He had a field representative who had dealt directly with the farmers in that area for many years and the manager of a similar buying station in the eastern part of the state. He had a transportation specialist, a construction engineer, a person from finance, and a retail merchandizing expert. They were meeting to think together where the new installation should be and how it should operate.

Ortega and his group set out the requirements of an ideal buying station and developed a pool of possible locations. They discussed the various sites, evaluating them against their criteria, and picked a location in the underserved, sparsely settled northwestern corner of the state, the crossroads village of Blanton, population 280. They selected Blanton because it sits in the center of a cluster of small wheat farms on a network of good farm roads and can be easily reached by truck from a main highway twenty-five miles to the south. Having agreed on the site, the group needed to design the package of goods and services the station would offer, in addition to grain buying.

Their criteria included the following items:

- Offers items and services related to grain buying and farming
- Offers items and services not readily available in the area as a convenience and inducement to farmers

"What's the best way to meet these requirements?" Ortega asked. Mack, the field rep, said that Blanton was in a marginal area, with occasional bumper crops and the constant threat of crop failure from drought, hailstorms, pests, and diseases. "People make a living out there, but they sometimes have to take in their belts," he said. Laura, from Finance, said that farmers always paid their bills but sometimes had to go for long periods on credit while their grain sat in the storage elevator at Tolbert, fifty miles away, waiting to be sold. Mack said Mrs. Ferguson, who operated the little general store in Blanton, was always pinched for cash because people had to buy on credit during part of the year; she had to buy her stock on credit, which was expensive for her since she was paying the interest costs for everyone.

Stevens, the retail merchandising man, said that the town needed everything since the nearest other store was at Winwood, a town of slightly more than 1,000 people sixteen miles away. "And it isn't much better than the general store in Blanton. The nearest decent stores are at Tolbert, about 5,000 population, more than an hour's drive away," he noted.

"They need all kinds of services, especially hardware, tools, and farm supplies," said Mack. "If something breaks down or runs out, if Bandy the blacksmith can't fix it or Mrs. Ferguson doesn't have it, it's a half-day trip to Tolbert, and that's murder during the harvest season." Geroux, the manager of the buying station in east Kansas, said, "But we can't do much about that without getting overextended. If there's one thing I've learned, you don't get into a business you don't know anything about." Several others said that trying to do everything would be asking for trouble.

Ken, the engineer, took the discussion in another direction. "We're going to buy land at Blanton and put up our buildings and elevators anyway. Why don't we put up another cheap building and rent it to someone who'll put in a hardware store and maybe carry farm supplies? That way, we wouldn't have to run it ourselves."

"That would run Mrs. Ferguson out of business," said Mack. "People out there wouldn't like that. Olson, our rep north of there in Nebraska, says she's helped a lot of people when they were down and out and is a real pillar of the community." "So why not rent it to Ferguson and help her expand her business into hardware and farm supplies?" asked Geroux. "Their credit would be safe enough," said Laura, "because we'd have the collateral sitting right there in our elevators." "We could give her a loan to stock up and get started," said Stevens, the merchandising man. "And maybe we could do the same thing and put the blacksmith in the farm equipment and repair business," said someone else. "We get a full service center and don't have to operate it."

That's what Western Grains did. It built offices and storage facilities in Blanton and put up three extra buildings, one for Mrs. Ferguson's farm and general store, one for Tom Bandy, the blacksmith and machinery repairman, and one for the village of Blanton, to serve as a community hall and meeting place. A lot of new business came into Blanton, and Western Grains soon had to consider adding more buying and storage facilities.

Ortega focused the attention of his resource people on a clearly defined issue. He encouraged them to talk about the issue and to get their ideas cut out in the open where others could see and react to them. He collected a pool of ideas and visibly displayed and shared them, and that was invaluable because it stimulated more thinking and opened up new directions and possibilities.

One new idea can make possible a thousand more new ideas. We think of creativity as the putting together of old ideas into new forms and combinations. A pool of good ideas invites, encourages, and almost forces creativity to occur. And creative thinking about what to do—a new and better way of doing something beyond the ordinary—is what you want. By getting ideas out where everyone can see and understand them, you set the stage for the creative combination of old elements into new entities. You don't even need to have all your resource people there in person. What is important is that the good ideas get together and better ideas emerge as a result. That is what collaboration is all about and why it works so well in resolving problems.

Productive Modes of Thinking

All modes of thinking can be productive in creating a pool of best ideas. Some suggestions come from rational thinking. "We're going to be putting up our buildings and elevators anyway; why don't we put up another?" asked the engineer. Laura, from Finance, drew on her rational thinking to say, "We'd have the collateral sitting right there in our elevators." A lot of use was made of intuitive thinking; people assumed that Mrs. Ferguson would welcome the chance to expand her business and put it on a solid financial basis, that Bandy would go for the idea of adding a mechanic and doing more on equipment repair, that a new source of services and supplies would bring business to the buying station. And Geroux, the manager of the other station, drew on his imaginative thinking to envision the future and warn of the hazards of trying to do too much when he said, "You don't get into a business you don't know anything about."

It was all fantasy and make-believe at first; then it became more practical and down-to-earth. Then the planners asked themselves, "Isn't that logical, and wouldn't it really work?" Before they knew it, they had created a new combination of ideas and tested it against rational thinking and taken Western Grains in a direction never considered before. Collaboration among the people who knew about the problem led to a resolution that none of them could have predicted at the outset. The arrangement was so successful that Western Grains has repeated it several times since in similar isolated locations.

If those people hadn't sat down to put their heads together, Western Grains would have done something less effective in the old traditional pattern. If Ortega hadn't asked them to think about meeting specific requirements, the resolution they came up with would never have happened. Having those highly informed people together, committed to finding the best resolution possible and focused and thinking about the same thing at the same time, is what made the difference.

The raw material for excellent resolutions is out there, in the memories and minds of people you can reach. All you have to do is get the ideas together, by whatever means are available— meeting, casual conversation, telephone, fax, e-mail, or team computing. Out of this fund of knowledge and experience, judgment and imagination, new and better ideas will emerge. Point your resource people in the right direction, focus their attentions through the questions you ask, and listen to their answers. They will tell you more than you thought they knew. They will fill your pool of excellent ideas to the brim.

HOW TO DO IT

Ask your resource people, "What are the best possible actions or alternatives available for meeting the requirements we have set?" Use all the communication media you can—phone, fax, e-mail, team computing, casual conversation, or formal meeting—to gather ideas and knowledge about ready-made alternatives and to gather a pool of the best ideas from which to build your final resolution. To do this, you and your work group should follow these steps:

1. *Set the task.*
   "What are the best ways we know to meet these requirements?"
   This tells your group that the task is to come up with the best means possible to satisfy the requirements of an ideal resolution.

2. *Review the requirements for an ideal resolution.*
   "These are the requirements we have to satisfy to achieve the best resolution possible."
   Refer back to the things you said you had to repair, improve, correct, or avoid in order to reach the ideal resolution. These will be the issues to focus on in thinking about actions to take.
   "Are we all agreed that these are the things we have to get done?"
   Make sure that there is a shared understanding of the requirements. If there is any disagreement or confusion about the criteria, clear it up before moving on.

3. *Get out the best ideas for action, one requirement at a time.*
   "What are the best ways we know to meet this requirement?" *or* **"What is the alternative that would satisfy this requirement?"**
   Focus on one requirement at a time. Give your group time to think and express its ideas. Draw out and help those who have trouble putting their ideas into words.
   Encourage discussion and interaction.
   Give people time to talk about each requirement and their ideas about actions to satisfy it. The best and most efficient actions come about through discussion.
   Record ideas as they emerge, and make them visible.
   Use a chart pad or blackboard to record ideas and alternatives so that they will be visible to everyone and not get lost. Clarify

and restate ideas and alternatives as they evolve. Gather them to form the pool from which you will build your resolution. **Go through each requirement in the same way.**

4. *Avoid the premature rejection of ideas.*
   "Don't reject an idea until you've heard it out and fully understand it."
   Good ideas sometimes sound nutty when you first hear them because they may be poorly stated or out of context and their implications may be unclear. Encourage the speaker to describe the idea more fully and to help others understand it.
   "I'm not sure I understand that. Could you say more about it?"

5. *Encourage the combination of ideas.*
   "How can that idea be combined with some of these others?"
   "Can we put these two good ideas together?"
   Refer back to earlier ideas that have been recorded on paper or blackboard. Get people thinking about combining individual actions into packages or programs of actions.

6. *Encourage the exploration of new directions.*
   "Is there any other way we could do this?"
   "Is there a simpler, easier way to do this?"
   Get people thinking about different ways to satisfy the requirements. Encourage them to use their imaginations. Get the interaction of ideas going.

7. *Review the pool of ideas.*
   "Are these the ideas or alternatives we will draw from in working out our best resolution?"
   Go over the ideas you have recorded, and make sure all of them are understood and agreed upon.
   "Are there any others that should be added to the list?"
   Add any others that are suggested. Make any corrections or modifications necessary to ensure that the best thinking of your group has been captured.

8. *Agree on the pool of ideas from which you will draw.*
   "Are we agreed that this is the pool of ideas or alternatives we will draw from in arriving at our best possible resolution?"
   Get positive agreement that these are the ideas from which you will draw. Make sure your colleagues understand the ideas and actions you have included in the pool.

Summary

Task 7 is to generate a pool of the best actions or alternatives your resource people can think of to meet your criteria. You take each requirement in turn and get your co-workers to think of ways to satisfy it, then encourage them to talk about it and build one idea on another to arrive at the best action possible for dealing with the problem. You challenge the group to find new and better ways to handle each issue by the questions you ask.

The steps in Task 7 are:

1. Set the task.
2. Review the requirements for an ideal resolution.
3. Get out the best ideas for action, one requirement at a time.
4. Avoid the premature rejection of ideas.
5. Encourage the combination of ideas.
6. Encourage the exploration of new directions.
7. Review the pool of ideas.
8. Agree on the pool of ideas from which you will draw.

Now you are going to pick out the very best of your best ideas and put them into a practical plan of action. Evaluating and selecting the best possible actions is Task 8.

13

Task 8:
Creating a Balanced and Workable Program of Actions vs. Just Doing It

Task 8 is to pick the best of the possibilities that have been assembled in your pool of good ideas and put them into a plan of action that will resolve your problem. Your task is to think carefully about what you need to accomplish and to select carefully the means you will use. This approach is in contrast to the tendency of some managers to settle for the first "good" solution that comes along.

"I say, let's just *do* it!" they proclaim, and then they charge into action. That could have been what Lord Cardigan said as he ordered his men into the action that later became known as the Charge of the Light Brigade. He had very little information and had received vague orders from his general. He had only one thing in mind: to charge the Russians at the end of a U-shaped valley stretching before him. With no planning and very little thinking, he just did it. It didn't work out very well for Lord Cardigan then, and that kind of decision making won't work any better for you now.

The commanding general couldn't see the lines of cannon, some 300 of them, on the hills overlooking both sides of the valley; neither could Cardigan, who commanded the Light Brigade. They both dismissed reports of the Russian guns, told to them by subordinates who had seen them. Because they themselves couldn't see the guns, they concluded that they weren't important. They didn't consider alternatives, didn't ask questions, didn't find out what their subordinates knew. They were Lords and generals and didn't care much what their subordinates thought about anything.

So Cardigan said, "Let's *do* it!" and made a suicidal charge into what became the worst slaughter of the Crimean War. If he had looked at a map of the ground or asked a few questions, things would have turned out differently. As it was, of the 700 men who started the charge, only a scant hundred were alive fifteen minutes later.

Your task is to pick the very best actions you can from the possibilities available and put them into a plan that will work. You and your co-workers have set out the requirements of the action, the things that must get done to resolve the problem. To meet those requirements, you have collected the best alternatives and ideas from which to choose. Now, if you take the very best of these and put them together in a feasible plan of action, you will have the best resolution that can be achieved in the present situation.

Three Parts of the Task

This task consists of three separate parts, each of which has to be completed in order to achieve the highest quality resolution:

1. Select the very best action to meet each requirement from the many excellent ones in the pool.
2. Arrange the chosen best actions in a time sequence to form a rough plan of implementation.
3. Anticipate and correct the potential problems that may arise in the course of implementation.

Does this seem like a lot to do, just to resolve a problem? If you simply take the first actions that come along and run with them, you'll wind up investing more time and energy than if you take more care and do it right. And what will you have in the end? An incomplete resolution that will self-destruct and collapse at its worst and barely survive at its best.

On the management battlefield, every day someone says, "Let's *do* it!" And there is a charge into action, the wrong thing is done, and others pay the price. Afterwards, people shake their heads and say, "You can't win 'em all." But that's the poorest excuse for gross incompetence there is, next to "I didn't know it was loaded."

You can win 'em all if you get the information and think about what you are doing ahead of time, select the very best actions to make up your resolution, put them into a rough time sequence plan, and anticipate and correct the potential problems that are likely to arise during the course of implementation. If you do these things, you'll never have the office rumormonger discussing your failings by the water cooler. Carry out Task 8, and you will always make the best of whatever situation you face, no matter how bleak.

Remember the Charge of the Light Brigade. Get the information out where you can think about it and where your colleagues can see and react to it before you make up your mind to charge ahead. Consider your alternatives, correct any errors that may have occurred, and pick the best way to get the job done. If you suspect hidden dangers, ask questions, seek out the dangers, and change your plans accordingly. Then, when you know what the situation really is, charge in the right direction toward the right objectives.

Selecting the Very Best Action

You want the very best action available to satisfy each particular requirement you have set. That means selecting the action that gets the job done best and costs the least money, causes the least hurt and inconvenience, and offers the most favorable benefit-to-cost ratio. That is certainly common sense, and simple enough. The trick is to organize the data you have to show which idea or alternative does the best job of meeting the specific requirement and which is most efficient and costs the least in coin and pain. Finding the best trade-off between cost and benefit is a matter of experience, thought, and judgment.

There is no magic way to find the best course of action. You and your colleagues will have to think your way to a conclusion. Task 8 is your opportunity to put your collective thought and judgment to work to change the future. There may not be a magic formula, but if you collaborate with the people who know the most about the problem, you have the best chance of emerging with the best solution.

The visibility of information is most important. You and your colleagues will be putting together hundreds of ideas and judgments to arrive at your end conclusion. If you try to do this all in your head or verbally, you are going to overlook or lose some items that will later turn out to have been crucial. There are limits to how many ideas and judgments you can juggle at the same time. Go beyond those limits and you lose detail. You must get the key data out where everyone can see and react to them in order to arrive at a common understanding of what is the best way to go.

Focus is all-important. You and your co-workers must all deal with one thing at a time in order to go beyond the ordinary. Defining the requirements for an ideal resolution helps you do that. Instead of looking in all directions, trying to think of a dozen things at once, you are focused on meeting one requirement at a time. Successful collaboration requires that everyone involved understand and attend to the same thing at the same time. You find the best way of satisfying that and then go on to the next. When you have found the best way to handle each requirement separately, you can then put all the actions together.

Making Decisions to Reach a Resolution

In Chapter 12 we said that there are two types of decisions that can be made in the resolution of a problem. The first is a *design* decision, in which you are confronted with a problem that has no accepted resolutions waiting up there on the shelf for you to choose from. You have to design or construct the resolution yourself out of the most appropriate elements you have collected in your pool of best ideas. When you have selected the best ways of satisfying each individual requirement and combined them in an integrated package, you have created the best plan that you can make for resolving that particular problem.

The second type of decision is a *choice* decision. In this case, the resolution involves choosing the best off-the-shelf, already-packaged-and-existing set of elements to meet the criteria, such as the best computer, plant site, or candidate for a job. You don't have to create the resolution from scratch; it already exists, and all you have to do is find it. You simply choose among several alternative packages, programs, or entities, judging each against the set of criteria you have already agreed upon, to determine which, on balance, does the job best for you. You ask "Which of these options will most nearly satisfy all of the criteria, taken as a unitary set of requirements?" You are searching for the best fit of an existing entity, thing, or program of actions to the specific pattern of needs you have identified.

Designing a Better Way

Hansen Wood Products, located on the West Coast of the United States, sells a broad selection of wood products nationwide. For years, Hansen followed the industry practice of producing an item and then finding a buyer for it. If, for example, it had fifty carloads of exterior plywood sheeting, salespeople across the country would be notified that the plywood was available and would call prospective buyers. The plywood would start a rail journey east in the meantime. If a salesperson found a customer who would buy a carload at the offered price, a railroad car would be shunted off, and the rest of the train would continue on.

This practice, known as auction selling, led to price cutting and special deals as each salesperson tried to underbid everyone else in the industry to get rid of the plywood at a marginal profit before it moved into someone else's region. Nobody made much money, and sales costs were high as people in the field repeatedly called on the company's more than 40,000 customers, trying to sell them some of the company's thousand or more products. Carloads of plywood and other products sometimes went all the way to the East Coast unsold, then turned around and headed west again before finding buyers. This floating inventory often contained items that few customers wanted, and production and shipping schedules often had to be changed to meet a customer's demand for something else.

Lee Baker, head of market planning for Hansen, considered this way of selling inefficient and decided to improve it. He and his staff invited a dozen field people and a dozen customers to a collaborative brain-picking session and asked for their opinions about what was wrong with the existing system and what an ideal one would look like. Over and over, those present expressed a need for reliable supply and stable prices. What could Hansen do to meet these requirements? A lot of suggestions were made, most to the effect that a continuing relationship based on each customer's needs would give both Hansen and the customer a chance to manage better and save money.

When the best ways for accomplishing the requirements were discussed and the best ideas were pulled together into a rough draft of a marketing program, it was apparent that a long-term contract with each customer, based upon its unique needs, would satisfy the requirements for an ideal system. So Hansen reorganized its entire marketing effort by selecting its top 2,500 customers out of its list of 40,000 and dropping the rest, offering each of the preferred customers a contract for Hansen to supply all wood products needs for the next year at a fixed price per item. Arriving at a one-time agreement instead of calling the customer every few days reduced Hansen's sales costs by 60 percent, and the increased certainty allowed production to carry out longer runs and more efficient scheduling. This enabled Hansen to offer better service at lower prices and still make a much better profit than it ever had before.

Hansen's customers were delighted to see a more predictable, orderly, and profitable business emerge as a result of the contracts. Everyone benefited. Lee Baker and his staff had not simply fixed something that was broken or repaired something that was performing poorly; they had used the ideas of people who knew about the problem to go far beyond the ordinary to design and create a new way of doing business. Hansen Wood Products sold out its full capacity under the new plan and expanded, while other suppliers in the industry were cutting back.

Making a Choice Decision

An earth-moving equipment company called Drexco sells several hundred types of machines and thousands of parts and offers a vast catalog of supplies. Drexco wanted to equip 375 of its salespeople with laptop computers that would provide instant information on everything in the company's line, enable the salespeople to place and confirm orders in a matter of seconds, and contain a database that would enable each sales rep to follow the progress of hundreds of contracts and deals-in-the-making, access the catalog, and obtain information about the company's leading competitors as needed.

Dozens of computers were available that could send and receive data through modems linked to phone lines and store and retrieve information. All had roughly equivalent processors, memory capacities, and other basic features. Yet all were different in end capability and price. Which of these was the best for the company's purpose? Computer salespeople were no help, because they tended to talk about the features their particular products offered. So Drexco formed a small group, headed by Denise Gregg, to study the problem and to recommend a computer to the board of directors.

Gregg and her working group carried out an analysis of Drexco's own needs (Task 6, as described in Chapter 11). They found that what the computers could do was far more important than the features. They refined their criteria of selection to eight performance requirements and attached weights of importance to each, using a scale of 1 to 10. The best computer for them would be the machine that performed best, on balance, at meeting all of the requirements. Here is the list of criteria they settled on, with the assigned weights of importance:

Reliability	10
Service available from manufacturer	8
Processor capable of supporting advanced software	8
Size of RAM and hard-drive memory	5
Screen visibility in ordinary light	4
Battery life	3

Weight   1
Price   7

Reliability was ten times more important than Weight, according to the list; next most important were the availability of service and the capability of the processor.

Gregg and her group next defined minimum standards of performance and modem compatibility and narrowed the alternatives to a pool of fifteen models that would meet or exceed those requirements out of a field of nearly forty. This brought them to the completion of Task 7, assembling a pool of best possibilities (see Chapter 12). But they still hadn't determined which would be the computer for Drexco.

They gathered the information that was available to determine which computer best met their criteria. A reputable computer magazine carried the results of a reliability survey of 70,000 users. These data were confirmed by discussions with two major repair facilities. A rating of the quality of the after-sale service rendered by different manufacturers was obtained. Technical data were collected about the processors employed and the RAM and hard-drive capabilities. The group carried out its own tests of screen visibility. Information on battery life and weight was available from dealers. And a firm, deeply discounted contract price for 375 units was obtained for each of the models. It wasn't hard for the group to collect the information it needed once it had decided what was important.

Gregg and her group organized all of this information in a single table comparing the fifteen candidate models. They discussed the performance of the candidates against the requirements and assigned scores to express their judgments, again using a 1–10 scale. Figure 13-1 presents the data they gathered for three of the fifteen models.

The ideal computer would meet all the requirements. But none of the machines was perfect. The first choice would therefore be the one that came closest. Gregg and her group had to weigh the benefits and disadvantages of each model in a way that allowed for a fair comparison; hence the need for a scoring system that would measure performance against a common scale of values. They had to judge, for example, how important

Figure 13–1. Comparison of computer models.

Requirements	Wt.	Model A	Model C	Model J
Reliability	10	86% Above Avg. 7 (70)	95% Best 10 (100)	78% Average 5 (50)
Service Quality & Availability	8	87% Very Good 8 (64)	96% Excellent 10 (80)	76% Average 5 (40)
Processor Capability & Speed	8	486 DX-2 8 (64)	DX-4 75 10 (80)	486 DX-2 8 (64)
RAM & Hard-Drive Memory	5	8mb-390mb 10 (50)	8mb-340mb 8 (40)	12mb-260mb 7 (35)
Screen Size Visibility	4	9.5" Good 10 (40)	9.5" Good 10 (40)	8.4" Fair 8 (32)
Battery Life	3	6.95 hrs 10 (30)	6.54 hrs 9 (27)	5.56 hrs 6 (18)
Weight	1	7.2 lbs 10 (10)	7.2 lbs 10 (10)	8.2 lbs 7 (7)
Price	7	–20% $3,429 8 (56)	–25% $4,461 4 (28)	–17% $3,236 10 (70)
Weighted Scores		(384)	(405)	(316)

the lower reliability of Model J was factored against its more attractive price and then to compare that judgment with the higher reliability and the sharply higher cost of Model C. They evaluated the performance of each machine against each criterion and then multiplied performance scores by the previously assigned weight to produce a weighted score. They then added the weighted scores to produce a total weighted score for each computer. The computer with the highest weighted score would be the one that performed best, on balance, against all the requirements.

"Is this numerical scaling necessary?" you ask. Yes, if the decision has much complexity. People say, "The devil is in the details," and that is so. The details often make the decision. A slight advantage here, a disadvantage there, a problem somewhere else, all add up and determine which option is best. When a lot of details are involved, you can lose track of how alternatives compare and of the judgments you have already made. When alternatives are close in desirability and there are a lot of details to consider, use some sort of scoring system. The numbers won't dictate the decision for you, but they will help you keep track of the many comparisons and judgments you are making.

Gregg and her working group presented their findings to the board and recommended the Model C. When questions were raised, they were able to show how they had made their judgments because they had the best ideas of the people they had collaborated with to draw upon. The board members were able to understand the recommendation and how Gregg and her people arrived at the conclusions they did. The presentation and discussion took only twenty-five minutes, and the recommendation was unanimously accepted.

Computer software is available to make choice decisions like this easier and more understandable.[1] It provides a number of ways to set criteria, assign weights, collect and display alternative information, compute preference scores, and print the whole thing out in an easily comprehended report. The software is particularly valuable if a large volume of detailed information is involved, many criteria must be considered, and the differences between alternatives are slight. It keeps all the facts and judgments straight so that nothing gets lost and no important bit of information is neglected. It would have fit perfectly with Gregg's approach, although she did her work manually in the actual case.

Forming a Rough Plan for Implementation

A decision is not complete when you decide on a program or alternative. That is only a first step toward a decision. The decision is complete only when you have set out a practical plan for its implementation and have anticipated and avoided the potential problems that might prevent it from succeeding.

This is true for both design and choice decisions. Once the actions for a design decision have been selected, they must be put together into a rough plan, a sequence of actions through time that will get the job done. What comes first? What actions depend upon other actions having already been taken? What actions can be taken simultaneously? Other supporting and enabling actions may also be necessary to make it all work out.

For a choice decision, steps have to be taken in time sequence in order to implement the decision. Supporting and enabling actions also have to be put in place to make it work. A rough plan puts it all together so that you can look at your proposed actions and make adjustments. Until you have a rough plan, you have only a statement of what you intend to do.

Consider the case of Brownlee Engineering and the carbon filament rocket bodies (see Chapter 10). Separations between the layers of carbon filament in the finished rocket body began appearing after six months of acceptable production. Hammond and his group found that the separations were occurring because not enough Teflon was being left on the molds to provide an adequate slipcoat. This made it necessary to use excessive extraction pressure to pull the rocket body off the mold, thereby tearing the wall layers apart internally. The resolution Hammond and his group created was to make it easier to be sure that enough Teflon was being deposited on the mold by coloring the Teflon blue so that operators could see that it hadn't settled out as the slipcoat was applied, that enough had been sprayed on the mold, and that buffing had not removed too much of it.

Hammond and his working group, plus a few of their resource people, listed the things that would have to be done to implement the resolution. In general, the list was generated in the order that the events would take place, but not always. Several times, actions that might have been brought up earlier in the process were thought of later on and had to be added. "Oh-oh, we forgot this one" was the way most of these came up.

The list contained items such as "report resolution to management and engineering, and get their OK," "get Purchasing to issue a special rush order for blue-colored Teflon slipcoat," "inform operators of cause of problem and new actions to be taken," and "generate quality standards for applying blue Teflon slipcoat." Supporting actions such as "provide extra supervision to see standards are met" and "inform prime contractor that the problem cause has been found and corrective action is being taken" were also added.

This list became a draft program of actions to be taken, with events strung in a sequence through time, like beads on a string. Common sense and good judgment were the guide. Approval from management had to come before Purchasing could issue a rush order for the new blue Teflon, for instance. The list was a first draft that would lead to a plan; its purpose was to get all the actions out in the open so that everyone could see the outlines of the new program.

Managers have to take two different, opposing roles when searching for the best resolution possible. They have to be optimistic and positive when trying to come up with ways to get something done; they also have to be pessimistic, cynical, and suspicious when they look at what they have just done and try to find something wrong with it, what won't work. In the old Western movies, the good guys all wore white hats and were optimistic and positive, while the bad guys wore black hats and were devious and cynical. Managers have to wear white hats when creating a resolution and black hats when searching for flaws and mistakes in what they have done; they then put on the white hats again when repairing these plans and making them better. They have to be able to be 100 percent white hat, then 100 percent black hat, then 100 percent white hat again in order to create the best plan possible.

After Hammond and his group put together their rough plan of action, they took off their white hats and put on their black ones, asking, "What could go wrong with this?" The operators immediately said, "There's a holdup in Purchasing, and we don't get the blue Teflon for weeks, so we have to use the stuff we have. We need special procedures to prevent more voids." "Yeah, and how blue will the Teflon be? Will making it blue really work?" And so on. Possible holes were seen in the plan in a dozen places.

"Okay," said Hammond. "What are we going to do about it?" So everyone put on his white hat again and began to think of ways to plug the holes: "We need to stir the slipcoat continuously so that the Teflon doesn't settle out, keep it looking milky"; "We can scratch the slipcoat on the mold in a few places to see that it's thick enough"; "We can hold back on the buffing and make sure we don't take too much off." A number of interim actions were suggested that would ensure enough slipcoat left on the mold to reduce extraction pressures. Standards and procedures were devised to make these stop-gap measures work. The revised rough draft of the plan was much more complete as a result.

Any plan must go through a process of generation, inspection, and improvement before it can be considered adequate. People are not capable of putting together a perfect plan the first time around, regardless of how experienced they are. There are too many details, interconnections, and unexpected effects. When a plan is made, any manager who intends to go beyond the ordinary must assume that it is incomplete and holds a lot of hidden threats and oversights; the manager must take responsibility for correcting those as part of her job. Switching from white hat to black hat and back to white hat is a powerful tool for getting that done.

Putting together a rough plan, then searching out its weaknesses and correcting them, uses both rational and intuitive thinking. You use your rational and intuitive modes of thought to set out what you want to happen in a logical sequence. You and your work group draw on your knowledge and experience to assemble the actions that have worked in the past and are most likely to work now. If you have drawn on a group of the best-informed people, you probably have access to 97 percent of what is known, available, and useful.

When you ask, "What could go wrong with this?" you are calling on intuitive thinking. You and your group will dig into experience and memory to come up with possible errors and oversights. Some imaginative thinking may enter in as well: "If this happened, then maybe that would take place." Listen to what comes out. Some ideas will be improbable, but most will be grounded in reality and very much worth considering.

When you put on the white hat and ask, "What can we do about this?" you and your group will use intuitive and imaginative or creative thinking again. Applying past experience to the present situation, someone will say, "Why couldn't we do this?" Then someone else will add another idea, and you will build upon a network of avoidance and preventive actions. Last, you will use rational thinking to test how practical these actions are.

White hat, black hat, white hat. Rational, Intuitive, Creative, Rational. Encourage your colleagues to use their minds, experience, and ingenuity; lead them by asking questions and assure them you want to hear their ideas. They'll get real satisfaction from doing it, and they'll provide you with resolutions that will enable you to go far beyond the ordinary.

HOW TO DO IT

Ask your colleagues, "What is the best plan of actions or alternatives to resolve this problem?" Bring your resource people together through whatever media you have available to evaluate and choose among the available ideas and alternatives to create the best resolution possible. Then ask them to find anything wrong with the plan and to correct it. As you work through Task 8, you will follow these steps:

1. *Set the task.*
   "What is the best program of actions or the best alternative to resolve this problem?"
   This tells your work group that the task is to pick the best group of actions or single alternative to meet your require-

ments and to integrate them into a rough plan for an ideal resolution.

2. *Review the pool of best ideas or alternatives.*
   "These are the best ideas or alternatives we have found to achieve the best resolution possible."
   Review your pool of the best ways to meet your requirements. These will be the elements on which you will draw to make up your plan for a resolution.
   "Are we all agreed that these are the best ideas we have to work with?"

3. *Select the actions that should be taken.*
   "What are the best actions to meet this requirement?"
   If you are creating a resolution through a design decision, help your resource people pick out the best action to satisfy each individual requirement.
   "On balance, which is the best alternative to meet all the requirements we've set?"
   If you are achieving a resolution through a choice decision, help your colleagues select the best alternative to satisfy all the requirements.
   Record all suggestions and make them visible.
   Get the group's ideas, and make them visible on some display medium. Use a scoring system to record judgments and to assign values.
   "Are we agreed that these are the best ways or the best alternative to do the job?"

4. *List all the actions that will have to be taken.*
   "What are all the things we will have to do to resolve the problem?"
   List all the actions that will have to be taken, including supporting actions required to make the resolution work.
   "Is there anything more we will have to do?"
   Probe for additional actions, particularly supporting actions, that may have been overlooked.

5. *Place these actions in time sequence and form a rough plan.*
   "Now let's make a plan. What has to be done first?"
   Arrange the actions in rough time sequence. Make sure support and enabling actions are included. Continue to look for other support actions that need to be taken.
   "Have we left anything out?"

6. *Anticipate possible problems in implementing the plan.*
"What could go wrong? What problems could we have in putting this plan into effect?"
Put on your black hats, and look for potential future problems in implementing these actions and make them visible.
"Are there any others we might have missed?"
Lead your group back over the plan, and look again for possible problems of implementation.

7. *Find ways to avoid or correct possible future problems.*
"What can we do to prevent or avoid these possible problems?"
Put on your white hats again, and look for ways to prevent, avoid, or reduce the effects of possible future problems.
"Is there anything else we can do to make our plan better?"
Lead the group back over the plan to look again for anything that could be added or changed to make it better.

8. *Restate your rough plan, and get agreement.*
"This is our rough plan for the resolution of the problem."
Restate the plan. Make sure that your co-workers share a common understanding of it. If there are any misunderstandings or disagreements, clarify them now.
"Are we agreed that this is a plan we can all work with and support?"
Get positive agreement from everyone involved.

Summary

Task 8 is to pick out the best possibilities that have been assembled in your pool and to put them into a rough plan to resolve the problem. You search for possible future problems of implementation and find ways to avoid or correct them, and then you encourage your group to dig into its experience, discuss its ideas, and make full use of all media and modes of thought. You lead the group to do these things by the questions you ask and by following these steps:

1. Set the task.
2. Review the pool of best ideas or alternatives.

3. Select the actions that should be taken.
4. List all the actions that will have to be taken.
5. Place these actions in time sequence, and form a rough plan.
6. Anticipate possible problems in implementing the plan.
7. Find ways to avoid or correct possible future problems.
8. Restate your rough plan, and get agreement.

Now you need to fine-tune your plan so that it has the greatest possible chance of success. You need to simplify, sharpen it, and make it as efficient as you can. This will be Task 9, your final opportunity to make your resolution as near the ideal as can be.

Note

1. *Decision Pad*, Apian Software, P.O. Box 1224, Menlo Park, Calif.

14

Task 9:
Fine-Tuning the Plan
vs. "It's Good Enough"

Task 9 is fine-tuning the plan so that it is as good as it can possibly be—not just good enough but as good as you and your colleagues can make it. Your task is to look at your plan from every angle to find every weak spot and to adjust and improve it until it is as near the ideal as possible. It is never "good enough" until it is as good as you and your people, with all your knowledge and creativity, can make it.

Making an outstanding plan is like crafting a fine sword hundreds of years ago. To make the sword, high-quality raw materials were assembled to forge the best steel, which is equivalent to what you did in Task 7 when you collected the best ideas available. Collecting the best raw materials was followed by the rough work of forging, hammering and shaping the blade; you took a similar step in Task 8 when you pounded out a rough plan for the resolution. Finally, grinding, sharpening, and polishing transformed the rough blade into an elegant work of the armorer's art and made the difference between a crude weapon and an outstanding one that balanced in the hand and cut through anything in its way. That is what you do in Task 9 of achieving a resolution that goes beyond the ordinary: make *your* plan a precise weapon to resolve the problem totally.

To do this, you and your colleagues must rework the plan to buff out its imperfections and rough spots. You go from white hat to black to white, searching for the plan's weaknesses and correcting them, simplifying and sharpening, emerging with a program of actions that will work without a hitch. Not all managers do this. Many stop with the rough blade when a little more care would have produced a superior product. They say the plan they produced on the first pass was good enough. Then they claim to be surprised and blame someone else when the plan fails to do all they hoped it would.

The essence of the task is to go from white hat to black to white again—to strive for the best actions, inspect the plan to find what is wrong or could be made better, then correct and improve the plan to eliminate the defects. The armorer wanted his sword to be perfect, so he felt along the blade for hidden imperfections that he could correct. If he weren't honest enough to admit there might be an imperfection and strong enough to search for it and correct it, he would never have created the work of art of which he was capable. Similarly, if you don't search for things to improve in your plan, there will always be weaknesses that you could have corrected if you had tried.

The Search for Weaknesses

The first step in fine-tuning your plan is to examine it for weaknesses. Some aspects of any plan are stronger than others.

In a design decision, where you put your best actions against individual requirements, the weak spot is the action you are uneasy about: "It's not perfect, but it's still the best we've been able to come up with." Give it another try, some extra attention. Focus people's efforts on it: "Isn't there something more we can do about this?" Let them turn their imaginations and creativity loose on the weak spot, and you may find there is indeed something more that can be done.

Many times, the weak spot is not the action itself but its implementation. If that is the case, focus people's attention on how the plan will be put into effect. What can you do to make sure the action is installed right so that it will work? Point your co-workers toward the weak spot in the plan and let them talk about it. They'll come up with new ideas that will make it work.

Thinking up the simple and efficient idea is hard work, and people tend to stop before they have exhausted all possibilities. The first ideas suggested are almost always complex ones. We don't know why, but experience tells us this is so. "Color the Teflon blue" wasn't the first idea to ensure that the slipcoat on the molds would be thick enough. It came later, after more complex suggestions had been made. Similarly, it took years for the idea of the shock-absorbing bumper and the crash-absorbing frame to be incorporated into the design of cars. They were added because someone said, "What we have isn't good enough. That's a weak point in our design." People thought about it, and someone else said, "Maybe if we tried this. . . ." Black hat opens the door for the white hat to come up with a winning idea.

The job of the leader is to direct attention toward fine-tuning the plan. People will know what to do once they get started. Your job is to see that they understand the importance of fine-tuning and do it. To lead them, ask questions that get them sharpening the same thing at the same time; prod them with questions so that they look for weaknesses. That's all there is to it, but it won't happen if you don't lead them into it.

In a choice decision, finding the weaknesses is easy. Look for the areas in which the final choice received low performance scores when you were making your comparisons among alternatives. Your best alternatives scored 10 or 9 or 8 on most of the criteria, but they possibly achieved only 3 or 4 on other requirements. Those low scores stand out like a neon sign. If you ask people, "How can we change this low-scoring alternative so that it does a better job against this criterion?," after a little discussion, someone will suggest how to modify it, substitute one action for another, or add a new action. The answer was there all the time. You had only to focus on the weakness to get it out.

Analyze the Strengths

If you can identify the strongest aspects of your plan and figure out what makes these parts of the plan so effective, you may be able to generalize from this and strengthen other parts of the plan as well.

One company was installing quality procedures on an auto assembly line. A line manager saw the lack of motivation among his workers to use the new procedures as a serious potential problem. "That won't be any problem on my line," said another line manager. "Why?" "Because they'll be able to see that the new procedures work and make the job easier for them." It turned out that workers on the second line would have visual evidence of success in front of them and would be motivated by the results, something that wouldn't happen for the other lines because the results of the procedures would be less visible for them. They would be doing something different only because their supervisor told them to, without knowing what difference it would make. So the procedures were changed to provide each working group with immediate feedback as to the results and benefits achieved, and a serious future problem was avoided.

Simplify the Plan

You and your colleagues should ask whether there is some way to make your plan simpler. "Can we streamline it? Why do we have to do it this way?" Many procedures are followed because they've been done that way in the past, so of course they need to be done that way in the future to keep with tradition. Requirements have changed, yet the procedures go on forever. If you build them into your new plan without thinking about them, you will weigh down the plan with unnecessary red tape.

People who do things want to have them as simple and clean-cut as possible. They know that this reduces confusion and lets them accomplish more with less effort. So ask your people who have firsthand knowledge of the action, "Is there a less complicated way to do this?" They'll tell you. But they probably won't tell you anything if you don't ask. They are used to seeing things done the traditional way and go along with it because they have seen that change is often unwelcome.

Another way to encourage simplification is to ask, "How can this be done more easily?" This directs people's attention to the extra steps that make an action difficult or awkward. "How could we do this faster?" gets at the time-consuming elements

in the task or procedure. Still another way to stimulate simplification is to ask, "How could we do it cheaper?" Or turn the
question around: "What makes this so expensive?" If you suggest ways to achieve simplification and let people know that
their ideas will be listened to, they will respond.

One of our clients is an integrated manufacturing company
that produces a wide range of products, often on a short time
schedule. The company can shift from one product to another in
a matter of minutes. Sometimes a given line will produce ten
different products on the same shift. This requires close communication and coordination between departments. To facilitate
this, each day between 8 and 10 A.M., the plant manager, and his
nine department heads gather in a staff meeting to set the next
day's schedules, allocate the plant's resources, and deal with
problems.

This procedure worked well when the plant was small and
turned out fewer products. But as the operation became more
complex, frustration mounted. Much of the meeting time was
taken up by discussion of specific problems by two or three people, while the others sat around, waiting for the next problem to
be considered. Yet the cross-functional communication gained in
the meeting was essential. There seemed no alternative to spend-
ing the two hours, suffering the frustration, and getting as much
good from the meeting as possible.

Then the manager raised the question "How could we make
these meetings more efficient?" This led to a discussion of what
each participant got out of the meeting. They all named three
benefits: (1) getting up-to-the-minute information on operations,
(2) knowing who was responsible for doing what by when, and
(3) having an opportunity to report on progress and comple-
tions. The manager had identified the same three benefits, using
different words: (1) having an interchange of information about
operations, (2) discussing and assigning responsibilities, and (3)
hearing about the outcomes of actions.

The group simplified its procedure by limiting the staff
meeting to the discussion of operations, responsibilities, and
progress. Problems would be dealt with separately by those involved, and the plant manager could be approached directly if a
special problem arose. The new staff meetings lasted only thirty

minutes and accomplished the same three functions, and everyone got a lot more done.

Another way to simplify is to combine parallel actions by creating a hybrid action that meets several requirements at the same time by putting similar things together. If you ask, "Is there any way we can combine some of these actions?" people will shift their focus toward consolidation and think about comprehensive actions. You may find these easier to implement than independent actions. Whenever possible, look for opportunities to combine actions.

Obvious? All simplification is obvious when you look back on it. Why didn't they do that in the first place? Because of tradition, inertia, and a failure to look the problem directly in the face. Once the manager raised the question about the meetings, a simpler way of operating was easy to find. The answer was there all the time. Before the question was raised, however, it was out of reach. Simplification seldom happens by itself. It is achieved only if you seek it out.

Look for Cost-Effective Actions

The first actions suggested for any plan are likely to be the most expensive. When you ask, "Is there a cheaper way of doing this?" you turn people's thinking toward more economical and simple ways of doing things. Since you are always looking for the most for the least, you should always ask people whether they know of a less expensive way of doing whatever it is you want done. They know a lot of shortcuts that will accomplish the same thing at reduced cost.

One company sold and installed information processing systems at the customer's place of business. During the first two weeks the system was operational, the company kept an engineer on hand at the customer's office, just in case. Most of the time, nothing happened; if there was a problem, it was usually minor and could be resolved in a matter of minutes. The company felt that having the engineer on hand was a good service and made the customer feel secure; however, it was terribly expensive. The engineer sat around and was bored.

A manager asked, "Can we do the installation for less money?" "Sure, we can give the customer a guide so that he can solve his own problems and stop sending our engineers out to do nothing" was one answer. The installation people drew up a brief trouble-shooting manual that listed the most frequent problems (to their surprise, there were only a dozen) and their resolutions. They also set up a hot line that provided expert advice when needed. The customers were satisfied, the engineers got back to work, and the company saved more than $3 million the first year. If the manager hadn't asked the question, the company would still be sending its engineers out to twiddle their thumbs.

Assign Responsibility and Accountability

Another aspect of fine-tuning is making sure that someone is responsible for each thing to be done. No action should ever be an orphan without someone to shepherd it along. And someone should be accountable for every action so that if something goes wrong, you'll know whom to ask for information and, more important, when things go as they should, you'll know who gets the credit.

For most managers, responsibility and accountability are associated with blame. When there is a failure, the organization knows whom to put on the rack; when all goes well, usually nothing is said. That is dead wrong. When you manage beyond the ordinary, you are voluntarily taking action to obtain a better result. The main functions of responsibility and accountability should be to make sure that everyone knows when a good job has been done and who did it. When a plan assigns clear accountability, it provides a manager with a roster of those who can be depended on when the next problem comes up. But accountability goes far beyond that.

All the tasks that contribute to managing beyond the ordinary depend on collaboration among people. Success depends on people's motivation to contribute what they can to resolve the problem at hand. Collaboration will occur only if people want to cooperate and are willing to draw on their experience and knowledge and work together. And that will happen only if everyone gets to share the satisfactions and benefits that come from success. If responsibility and accountability are used to reward and not just to punish, you can move beyond the ordinary time after time. If nobody gets credit for collaboration, there won't be any the next time you need it. Collaboration is *given*, not extracted; accountability and reward go hand in hand, and collaboration will not come to you unless you use both fully and fairly.

Make a Final Search for Potential Problems

The last step in fine-tuning any plan for action is to conduct a risk analysis, a final search for potential future problems that might prevent the plan from succeeding. A plan is a program of change, and change leads to new results that can become new problems. Thus, the black hats go on once again.

Look at the Mechanics of the Plan

The first place to look for possible future problems should be the plan itself. Is it complete? Does it flow along, or does it have rough spots? Are there points where many activities come together, where coordination might break down? Do some people have too much to do and others too little? Is the timing realistic? Are the people involved provided with the information and resources they need? Are there any weaknesses left unresolved? Are there any loose ends? Has anything been overlooked, assumed without verification, or just plain forgotten?

This first look has to do with the mechanics of the plan, the details of how it is intended to work. A good way to do this is to talk it through and give it a dry run in the presence of people who know about the issue and are looking for mistakes and glitches. "Wait a minute," a participant might say. "What makes you think this will happen the way you say?" This is a signal to dig in and check whether an assumption has been made without a basis in fact. Shake the plan, inspect it, and turn it upside down. If you find just one flaw or weakness, the effort has been worthwhile.

Look at Other Activities of the Organization

The second place to look is at how the plan will integrate with other activities of the organization. Does it serve the purpose of the organization? Does it conflict with anything else the organization is doing? Does it place anyone or any activity in a conflict of interest? Does it place an extra burden on any other part of the organization? Possible future problems involving the rest of the organization are often hard to see, are seldom questioned, and sometimes have deadly consequences.

If an activity is to succeed, it must mesh with everything else that is going on. If it doesn't, it may create new problems more serious than the ones it set out to correct. This requires another talking through. Where does this activity touch on other activities? Does it depend on another activity? Do other activities depend on it? What are the interactions between this activity and others in the organization? Don't assume that everything will work out all right in the end. The odds are against you. It is too easy to overlook something important that will cause trouble in the days to come.

Look at the Outside Environment

The third place to look for trouble is the outside environment. Will the plan conflict with activities, happenings, or conditions outside the organization? Will the world outside have an effect on it? What likely changes in the business, social, legal, or natural environment might have an impact on the plan? You need to look at the events and conditions that could hurt the plan most, such as costs, supplies, demands, legislation, and the activities of other organizations. Ask yourself, "What factors could most seriously hurt our plan? Can we expect changes in any of these?"

A company had an ambitious sales plan for a new product it was about to launch. At a risk-analysis session, someone asked, "What would happen if one of our major suppliers had a strike?" "Come on," said another. "That's too farfetched to bother with." "No, it isn't," said a third person, who named a sole supplier of an important item the company would depend upon. "They're having a lot of trouble about work rules." It turned out that a strike or other work stoppage was possible, even likely. The company contacted a second source, just in case. When a work slowdown did materialize at the first supplier, the company was ready and carried out its plans successfully. But if it hadn't raised the question, it would have been hurt badly.

Change is inevitable. You must anticipate changes that might affect you and your plans, or else someday you will be caught flat-footed. There is no reward in management for this. And you can't convince anyone you were innocent by saying, "I didn't know it was going to happen." The future is full of happenings. It is so easy to look ahead and ask, and so foolish not to. Forewarned is forearmed, as the old saying goes.

Some people will protest they don't like to think negative thoughts. Others will say that asking people to anticipate everything that can go wrong will stop progress, and nobody will do anything because of fear that a problem will crop up. Still others will say that this opens the door to fantasies and unlikely horror stories. But the greater horror stories are those in which no attempt was made to identify future difficulties when trouble was waiting around the corner and could have been seen had anyone looked. If you know what the threat is, you can deal with it; if you don't know, you can't do anything.

There is another side to this—opportunity. Not all change is threatening. Some changes provide opportunities you can take advantage of once you are aware of them. Look into the future and ask, "What is going to happen out there? Can we benefit from the changes that lie ahead?" While you are looking for future change, keep in mind that positive things can come from changed conditions. When you anticipate a future change, you can act either to defend yourself or to take advantage of an opportunity.

Fully use the experience and intuitive knowledge of your colleagues. Their memories are storehouses of information about what has gone wrong in the past and what might happen in the future. Encourage them to draw on everything they know, because most of it will be valid information. Face-to-face communication is excellent, but team computing, fax, and e-mail can be extremely useful as well. Your resource people will often be more candid and open when sending their thoughts across a wire than knee-to-knee with you and their other colleagues. Listen and you could learn a lot.

Take Action to Change the Future

Once a possible future problem has been identified, you can take two kinds of action—preventive and contingent.

Preventive action is action taken to neutralize or block off the cause so that the problem won't occur. A preventive action against fire in your office is the use of fireproof materials. You can prevent the cushions on your garden chairs from getting spoiled by the rain by bringing them inside. You act against the cause and remove it or put it out of operation. A preventive action is efficient because the possible problem has been eliminated.

Contingent action is taken to ameliorate the effects of the future problem if it should occur. A contingent action against fire is the purchase of a fire extinguisher. It doesn't prevent a fire from occurring, but it helps you control the damage if one does. You can take contingent actions against an earthquake by having food and water on hand and bolting your house to the foundation. Contingent action lightens or contains the effects of a problem so that you don't suffer as much injury as you would have if you had let nature take its course.

If you think about your plan, you and your colleagues can identify the most likely ill effects that might occur. Your experience tells you what is risky, potentially harmful, and likely to occur. Once you have identified these outcomes, you can devise preventive and contingent actions against them. You draw primarily on your intuitive knowledge for this task and rely less on your rational thinking. You and your group have heard a thousand tales of things that went wrong and a thousand accounts of what people did to deal with them. The experience and the imagination of well-informed people are the greatest sources of preventive and contingent ideas you can find. You cannot lose by identifying and taking action against potential problems. Every problem you deal with is one less problem you and your co-workers may have to suffer later on.

Actions to take advantage of an opportunity are contingent in nature. But you can't take advantage of future opportunities unless you look ahead.

Check Every Plan

The final search for potential problems is important. Every plan without exception should undergo a painstaking black-hat inspection, because every plan made by a human being contains some error or oversight. No threat is too trivial to consider, and an overlooked future problem may be about to explode on you at any time. Consider what happened to the Board of Supervisors for the city of San Francisco in 1994. They proposed renaming Army Street "Cesar Chavez Street" in memory of the late California agricultural labor leader. "Great idea . . . will please a lot of minority voters," they thought, so they enacted the change into law.

But Army Street is a long north-south thoroughfare that is used by many people and that intersects two major freeways. Nearly a hundred street signs would have to be changed in the most expensive way, since they would go from a very short name to a long one. There were also several monster signs that spanned freeways at the on-off ramps that would have to be changed. Because the new signs would need to be much larger to accommodate the longer name, they would require new, stronger supports, since San Francisco is in earthquake country. Maps would have to be changed, and letterheads, and the names of businesses, and on and on. The total estimated cost to the city of the name change came to $900,000. "But the real embarrassment came," said an article in the *San Francisco Chronicle*, "when it was learned that [the supervisors] never bothered to check out the potential sign cost before leaping to rename the street." Anyone, given five minutes of thought, could have listed a dozen consequences of changing the name of a much-used street. More than a year later, there were still hearings and protests about the name change.

It is a law of physics that every action has a reaction, which translates into a law of business, politics, and everyday life that every action has effects, among which is always cost. Most of the business catastrophes we hear about occurred because nobody asked, "What could go wrong?" or "What effect would the proposed change have?" We believe that 90 percent of the "surprises" we see around us every day, from business difficulties to social and political tragedies, could have been predicted if someone had taken the time and effort. And it doesn't take much of either. It takes the willingness to set aside your white-hat advocacy and to wear a black hat to question whether some wonderful plan or great idea might possibly contain some hidden flaw or shortcoming. Be safe. Give your plan a skeptical inspection. Find its flaws, errors, and oversights. Look for the changes that lie ahead. Then put on your white hat and go to work.

Get Agreement and Commitment

The last step in fine-tuning your plan is to obtain positive agreement that it is the best you and your group can create. If your colleagues don't agree that it is as good as they can make it and that they can work with it and support it, find out what the problem is and deal with it to get agreement.

No plan is complete until those who must put it into effect are satisfied that it will work and agree to try their best to make it work. To be successful, the people who must make it work must embrace it as a doable plan. Success then becomes a matter of pride and conviction. If they have contributed to it, they will do far more to make it succeed than if it is handed to them with instructions to get it done or else.

Any plan that lacks commitment from those who must make it succeed is incomplete. If you draw on the people who know the problem and have taken part in resolving it, you will automatically have their ownership and commitment because they have been involved in it from the beginning. It will be theirs, and they will make it succeed if they possibly can.

HOW TO DO IT

Ask your work group, "How can we make this plan better?" Bring them together to search out the weaknesses in the plan and to simplify and sharpen the plan to a razor edge. Lead them to fine-tune it by asking questions that focus their thinking on its improvement and on the prevention of future problems and by following these steps:

1. *Set the task.*
   "Our task now is to fine-tune our plan so that it is as perfect as we can make it."
   This tells your group that the task is to make a good plan even better and that they are the ones who can do it. This tells them that nothing short of the best is good enough.

2. *Search out the weaknesses.*
   "What are the weak points in our plan?"
   Review the plan, and evaluate how well its actions serve the requirements you set out to satisfy. Identify areas of weakness for subsequent improvement.
   "Which actions do a poor job of meeting this specific requirement?"
   For a design decision, examine how well each specific requirement has been satisfied, and identify those actions that could be improved.
   "Which elements in the best alternative score lowest in meeting the requirements you set out?"
   For a choice decision, identify the elements in the chosen alternative that satisfy the requirements least well and that could be improved.
   "How can we strengthen this action or element?"
   Encourage people to draw on their experience, knowledge, and creativity to come up with an improved, modified, or additional action or element.

3. *Analyze the strengths.*
   "What actions or elements do best in meeting the requirements?"
   Identify the outstanding performers or scorers in your actions or alternatives, and find out why they do so well.

"How can we apply that strength to other, weaker actions or elements?"
Identify what makes for that strength and how you can generalize it to other actions and elements in your plan.

4. *Simplify.*
"How can we make this action simpler?"
Get your group to think about how to reduce complexity and make a difficult action more streamlined and clear-cut.
"Less complicated? Do it faster? Cheaper? More easily?"
Describe simplification in different words that will focus the group's thinking on its different aspects. Make simplification sound like common sense and the natural thing to do.

5. *Combine actions.*
"How can we combine some of these actions and put them together?"
Lead your group to think about collapsing related actions into one action, making the plan more compact, practical, and manageable.
"Are these actions that can go together?"

6. *Find cost-effective actions.*
"Is there a cheaper way of accomplishing this action?"
A less expensive action suggests a simpler, less elaborate way of doing something. You always want the most for the least, without sacrificing quality.

7. *Assign responsibility and accountability.*
"Who should see that this step gets done?"
Every action should be the responsibility of someone. There should be no unsupervised actions in your plan.
"Who should be held accountable for the successful completion of this action?"
Accountability defines who gets the credit for success or the blame for failure. Everyone should know who is accountable for each portion of the plan.

8. *Search for potential problems and future opportunities.*
"What could go wrong with the mechanics of this plan?"
Look at the plan itself, and talk it through. Shake it, turn it upside down, and search for any hidden flaws.
"What could go wrong in the way the plan meshes with other activities of the organization?"
Look at how the plan serves the purposes of the organization

and how it is to be integrated with other activities to identify problems of coordination or conflict.

"What could change in the outside environment which would hurt our plan?"

Anticipate changes in the outside world that might affect your plan. Use fully the experience and the intuitive knowledge of your group.

9. *Take actions to change the future.*

"What can we do to prevent this future problem from happening?"

Get people to think of ways to neutralize or block the cause so that the problem can't occur. Draw on their experience, intuitive knowledge, and imaginations.

"What contingent action can we take if it does happen?"

Get the group to think of "what-if" actions it can take to deal with the problem if it does occur. Again, encourage your co-workers to use their experience, intuitive knowledge, and imaginations.

10. *Get agreement and commitment.*

"Do we all agree with this plan and support it?"

Get positive agreement that the plan is as good as possible and that all involved can support and work with it.

Summary

Task 9 is to fine-tune your plan so that weaknesses are identified and strengthened and possible future problems are recognized and either prevented or contained. To do this, you simplify and streamline the plan and encourage your colleagues to make the plan as good as it possibly can be. You lead them to do these things by asking questions and by following these steps:

1. Set the task.
2. Search out the weaknesses.
3. Analyze the strengths.
4. Simplify.
5. Combine actions.

6. Find cost-effective actions.
7. Assign responsibility and accountability.
8. Search for potential problems and future opportunities.
9. Take actions to change the future.
10. Get agreement and commitment.

Task 10, the final task, is to record and communicate your resolution to others so that they will understand it in the same way that you and your colleagues do. Your task is not complete until you have obtained their acceptance and support for the recommendations that you and your work group are making.

15

Task 10:
Communicating for
Acceptance vs. Just
Telling About It

You and your work group have created the best resolution to the problem that you can. Your final task is to communicate it to others so that they will understand it the same way you do and accept and support it. That is Task 10—to sell your ideas to the rest of the world so that your good thinking is used.

You and your co-workers have spent many hours reaching the conclusions you have, going through a mountain of information to arrive at your resolution. Now you have to communicate your recommendations to others who know less about the problem, are involved in other matters, and haven't much time to listen. Your goal is to have them accept your conclusions, believe in them, and do what is necessary to put them into effect.

If a resolution is not understood and accepted by the people authorized to put it into being, it is wasted, because it won't resolve or change anything. To be complete, it must be in place and actively improving the problem situation. Anything less is only a lot of words. A resolution has to do something to be genuine. That is why the final task is getting it understood and implemented.

Reporting Your Recommendations the Right Way

To win support and understanding for your resolution, it's necessary to report your recommendations so that they make good, practical sense and your listeners understand them. We learned the secret of this from a client who faced this requirement every day. His name was Jim Fogarty, and he and his colleagues studied problems for a government agency and developed recommendations to resolve them. They then presented their conclusions to a commission of elected officials, each with a personal political agenda. The commission would listen to the presentation, then vote to accept or reject the recommendations. Fogarty and his group made good recommendations, but only 30 percent of them were accepted; seven out of ten were argued about and lost in political squabbling. This made Fogarty and his colleagues unhappy, because they knew their recommendations were good and most should have been accepted. They wondered what they are doing wrong, why they didn't have a higher success rate.

We analyzed twelve recent cases in which their recommendations had been rejected. What had the arguments been that had scuttled their recommendations? It took less than two hours to determine that every recommendation had been lost because some part of the information or logic upon which it had been based had been left out or was not understood by the commission members. Wherever there was a hole in the recommendation, the officials supplied their own inadequate, scattered, and politically biased information, resulting in confusion and deadlock. This allowed politics and special interests to enter, along with personal conflicts and charges. The good recommendations by Fogarty and his people were lost.

"We have to make sure we present a complete story with no holes," Fogarty said when we finished the analysis. "Then maybe the commission will understand why our recommendations ought to be accepted." He set out the steps of a complete analysis, from the first recognition of trouble to the final plan for its resolution. These formed an outline for the group's presentations, which it used religiously from then on, to ensure that the logic of its analyses would be completely clear and leave no holes that others could exploit. The group went from having three out ten of its recommendations accepted to having eight out of ten accepted. The resolutions hadn't become better, but the way they were reported had. Now the commission members could follow Fogarty's logic, making it more likely that they would accept most of his recommendations.

If you are to convince your listeners that your resolution has merit, you need a complete, logical account of the information you have considered and the logic that led you to your conclusions. When you have carried out the tasks needed to produce a complete resolution, you have followed an unbroken stream of logic, and your conclusions make sense. If you present your recommendations using that same stream of logic, your report will make inarguable sense to your audience, because all the essential details and linkages will be there. That's what Fogarty and his group did, and it worked.

The Problem Resolution Report

When you have properly arrived at your resolution, a detailed account of the information and logic you used to do so has already been gathered. All you have to do is enter the answers to the questions you asked into a simple communication format. You already have that framework, which consists of the ten tasks and the questions they pose. The only other thing to do is to write a short cover memo.

Figure 15-1 presents the framework of an ideal Problem Resolution Report. It covers everything you need to cover and doesn't add anything you don't need. Anyone can read and understand it. You can put it into your word processor and use it as a form to be filled out with the details of your problem any time you have an issue to analyze and record. (You may wish to modify it to your particular needs.) It will do a large share of your communicating for you.

Referring to the people under him, one vice president of a Fortune 500 company told us, "I don't care if they come up with better resolutions or not. If they just give me reports like this, it's

Figure 15–1. Problem resolution report.

Date: Reporter:

Problem Name:

Manager: File #:

WORKING GROUP:

RESOURCE GROUP:

PROBLEM SITUATION:

PROBLEM DESCRIPTION: It IS   But is NOT

DEFICIENCY:

ON WHAT:

WHO:

WHERE:

WHERE ON OBJECT:

WHEN:

WHEN IN SEQUENCE:

UNIQUE FEATURES:

DIFFERENCES & CHANGES:

LIKELY CAUSE:

CONFIRMATION/PROOF:

REQUIREMENTS: ACTIONS or ALTERNATIVES:

PLAN: ACTIONS TO BE TAKEN: WHO RESPONSIBLE:

FINE TUNING: Simplify, improve, consolidate, countermeasures

RECOMMENDATIONS, FINAL PLAN:

worth the price of admission." He said he could quickly tell from the report what the problem and the recommended solution were, what had been done, and why the report's conclusions had been reached. He knew where the information he needed could be found; it was all there on a couple of pages. The report was orderly, brief, and clear, and it saved him time, energy, and aggravation. His staff soon found out that if it wanted a quick, favorable response, it was well advised to give him a report in this format. Of course, if the staff had done all the things called for in the report, it had reached a better resolution than it would have otherwise reached, so he couldn't lose.

The Ideal Report

Figure 15-2 presents a report on the problem of the voids in the rocket section walls experienced by Brownlee Engineering (see Chapter 10). It has been edited from the original to remove proprietary information and slightly simplified for clarity. The full plan to be implemented has been left off since it involved details that are neither relevant nor useful for our purposes.

Otherwise, this report accurately represents the one Herb Hammond and his people made to top management. This was a complex problem that had already cost Brownlee millions of dollars and gone on for months unresolved. Executives of the company had raised serious questions about the organization's ability to deal with carbon fiber technology. This report was a clear summary of what had gone wrong with the rocket project, why it had happened. The presentation was well received, the recommendations were accepted, and the actions taken. The voids disappeared, and the rocket project successfully moved ahead.

The first part of the report contains the date and identifying information, something any report should have. This tells the reader what he or she is looking at. Next are the names of the members of the working group and the resource group. This is important for three reasons. First, it tells the reader the credentials and expertise of those who contributed. Anyone reading the report knows at once that these are solid people who have

Figure 15–2. Problem Resolution Report at Brownlee Engineering.

Date: June 14, 1996   Reporter: David Williams

Problem Name: Voids in rocket body wall

Manager: Herb Hammond, Project Manager   File #: BA626

WORKING GROUP: Jim Dorner, Quality Engineering
Gary Taylor, Supervisor, rocket line
David Williams, Project Engineer

RESOURCE GROUP: Kevin Crosby, Operator, rocket line
Gene Franklin, Senior Quality Inspector
John Haynes, VP Graphite Technologies
Ken Johnson, Fiber Wrap Specialist
Tim McNerney, Kiln Operator
Bob Perdue, Chemical Engineering
Bill Reiser, Lead Man, rocket line
Connie Renn, Central Testing Lab
Steve Schecter, Purchasing
Ray Snyder, Operator, rocket line
Ruben Valdez, Materials Engineering

PROBLEM SITUATION: Voids appear between layers in graphite-resin rocket sections beyond size allowed in Spec. 147A2c, sub.9, substantially weakening structure, causing rejections by Quality Inspection, causing delivery delays and financial penalties.

PROBLEM DESCRIPTION:	It IS	But is NOT
DEFICIENCY:	Voids between layers in wall of graphite-resin rocket body section	Any other quality problem
ON WHAT:	Lower section, rocket body	Middle, upper sections
WHO:	Personnel, rocket line	
WHERE:	Inspection station, rocket line	
WHERE ON OBJECT:	1–2.5 ft. from lower end of section 3rd, 4th layer from inside	14.5–16 ft., upper part of section. Not outside 16–17 layers
WHEN:	First reported, ultrasound quality inspection station Voids started 5 weeks ago, continuing to present time	Not sporadic, all lower sections since first started
WHEN IN SEQUENCE:	After baking, cooling, after section removed from mold After 6 months production with no voids	

(continues)

Figure 15–2 (*continued*).

UNIQUE FEATURES:	Voids torn, not a lack of adhesion between layers Lower section most rigid, has most layers of graphite fabric, middle & upper sections more flexible, fewer layers of fabric Lower 1–2.5 ft. least flexible, thickest part of section Extraction machine attaches to section at lower end for removal from mold Last 4 lower sections produced rejected for voids
DIFFERENCES & CHANGES:	Size of Teflon particles in slipcoat increased 2 months ago Slipcoat "used to be milky, now it isn't" Extraction pressures increased 40% last 2 months "Buff to high gloss" order given 6 weeks ago
LIKELY CAUSE:	Not enough Teflon on mold, caused by too many Teflon particles settling out of slipcoat and removed by buffing, to prevent graphite fabric from sticking when pulled off, causing extraction pressures to rise, tearing graphite layers apart internally at point near attachment of extraction yoke to rigid, less flexible lower section of rocket body
CONFIRMATION / PROOF:	Extraction pressures up 40% after buffing order given Larger Teflon particles observed to settle out in 3 minutes, leaving clear lacquer carrier, providing insufficient lubrication Visual inspection demonstrates insufficient Teflon left on mold after buffing Lab simulation demonstrates elevated extraction pressure necessary when amount of Teflon reduced by buffing, causing internal rupture of graphite fabric

REQUIREMENTS:	ACTIONS or ALTERNATIVES:
Obtain plan approval	Presentation, communication, Brownlee top management
Keep Teflon in suspension	Return to earlier, smaller size Teflon particles less likely to settle out quickly Continuous agitation of slipcoat solution so that settling cannot occur
Make Teflon visible	Have Teflon particles dyed bright blue so can be seen in suspension, see how much deposited on mold Obtain, test, inventory colored Teflon slipcoat Generate new standards, minimum color of mold after slipcoat applied, before graphite fiber wrapped
Reduce buffing to minimum	Generate new standards for buffing Inspection: Amount Teflon required on mold after buffing
New slipcoat procedures	Establish gloss, colorimeter standards for adequate slipcoat deposit before graphite fiber winding Slipcoat quality inspection before winding Establish maximum safe extraction pressure standards
Relations with prime contractor	Presentation of analysis and corrective actions, prime contractor, and Brownlee engineering, sales, account people Presentation, Brownlee Legal Department

PLAN:	ACTIONS TO BE TAKEN:	WHO RESPONSIBLE:
	Presentation, Brownlee top management, get approval	J. Haynes, VP, Graphite Technologies
		H. Hammond, proj. mgr.
	Presentation, Brownlee Legal Dept., get approval	H. Hammond, proj. mgr.
	Generate specifications, new colored Teflon slipcoat	D. Williams, proj. eng.
	Presentation, prime contractor, Brownlee engineering, sales, account people	H. Hammond, proj. mgr.
	Order new Teflon slipcoat for test, inventory	H. Hammond, proj. mgr.
	Generate new standards, slipcoat deposit limits	J. Dorner, qual. eng.
	Generate new standards, slipcoat buffing	D. Williams, proj. eng.
	Order gloss meter, color measuring equipment	J. Dorner, qual. eng.
	Order continuous agitation equipment	S. Schecter, purchasing
	Determine maximum safe extraction pressure	R. Valdez, mtls. eng.

FINE-TUNING: Simplify, improve, consolidate, potential problems and countermeasures

Operator suggestion, continuous agitation can be obtained with existing equipment

Color refraction meter, used by operator, cheaper and easier

Potential Problem: Operators won't follow new procedures, actions will be ineffective.
Countermeasure: full information to operators about problem, reasons for new actions, get cooperation

Potential Problem: May be delays in getting new procedures to work.
Countermeasure: build ahead on lower section of rocket bodies, inventory for insurance against delivery delay

RECOMMENDATIONS, FINAL PLAN:

---

firsthand knowledge of the problem and whose ideas are worth considering. Second, it tells the reader who has contributed to the reward for purposes of reward and resource inventory. This is important because it identifies employees who are valuable because of their past collaborations and who might be expected to help in the future. Third, it provides direct satisfaction to those who have been involved in arriving at the resolution, since it acknowledges their efforts and sends a message to them and to the rest of the organization that the intelligence and the experience of ordinary people are valued and listened to.

The Problem Situation section gives a closely worded statement of what is happening. This provides the reader with an overall picture of the situation and makes it easier to understand what comes next.

The Problem Description section sets out the details of the problem. It uses the what-where-when approach that good journalists employ when they give a complete description of a happening. The problem description concentrates on what the problem is and what its boundaries are, what is relevant and what is not. This forces the reader to ask, "What's the difference? What's unique about one factor that isn't shared by the other?" This gets your readers thinking along with you, rather than second-guessing your conclusions.

Understanding the information included under the headings Differences and Changes, Likely Cause, and Confirmation and Proof leads your readers to the same conclusions that you and your colleagues have reached. Nothing hurts your presentation more than leaving your readers unconvinced. Knowing the cause and being able to prove it is the most convincing single thing you can do to sell your conclusions to others.

Having identified what the problem is and what caused it, you next consider what to do about it. The Requirements section, in which you present the criteria for an ideal resolution, forces your audience to analyze what the planned actions are intended to accomplish. It also limits the audience's thinking to what is relevant and keeps them from wandering off into tangential and confusing matters. When your readers understand and accept the requirements you and your colleagues have set, they will be predisposed to accept your conclusions. If they find a valid exception to a requirement or suggest a new one, you simply adjust your set of requirements accordingly and modify your analysis. This seldom happens, but when it does, it cements their commitment to the modified plan, since they have now contributed to it and feel personal ownership for it.

The same applies to the Actions or Alternatives section. If your readers understand and accept the actions or alternatives you and your co-workers have seen as appropriate, they will buy into your conclusions. If they come up with valid new actions, consider them and enter them into your analysis if worthwhile. If your readers have made a useful contribution, they will become part of the new conclusions you will reach and become champions for your cause.

When you move on to creating a Plan of Actions to be

Taken, your report allows your audience to evaluate how well a particular idea meets a particular goal and leads them to the same conclusion you have reached because they are using the same standards and logic you used. The only way they can arrive at a different judgment is to suggest a requirement or some information you have overlooked. Once your listeners enter into the logic of your report, they become captive to it and are led to its inevitable conclusions.

In the Fine-Tuning section, your report invites readers to enter into the plan along with you. As they go through the steps of searching for weaknesses and simplification and looking for more cost-effective actions or alternatives, the report preempts their asking, "Have you thought of this?" They are led to convince themselves that your recommendations are the most logical ones possible and the ones they would have made had they been in your shoes. It is a sales piece that puts them solidly on your side.

Picking Your Targets and Hitting Them

Shouting your message from a rooftop in the hope that someone will hear it or dropping 50,000 leaflets from a high-flying plane is not effective communication. Selecting the targets you need to hit, aiming at them, and scoring a series of bull's-eyes, on the other hand, are indeed effective communications.

Your targets are those who want to see the problem resolved and can do something about it—people who have a pet project, want someone to share their concern, and who will see your resolution as a help to them; people with the authority to approve, support, and implement your resolution; people who have the power to shake things up and give you a hand with your project.

There usually are only a few targets who are really important, eight or ten people at the most. If you and your working group give it a little thought, you can list the handful of people who are vital to your project and can make it succeed. You know who they are. They are the ones you need to convince.

To move these people, list the things they are most interested in that touch on your project. What do they think is important? What gives them the most satisfaction? What do they think is most in need of improvement? What concerns them the most deeply that your resolution might relieve? Study them, scope them out. Get your work group to discuss them. Ask people who know them well to help you. Find some tie between your project and the wants and needs of each of your targets.

When you have found a connection, talk with your resource people about how you can make some feature of your resolution seem like a gift from the gods to your target. How can some effect from your project move your target's interests forward and make life easier for him or her?

Remember our account of Hansen Wood Products in Chapter 13? Lee Baker and his people came up with a new way of selling that would save money, increase profits, and make it easier for Hansen's customers to manage their businesses. Great! But the new method would mean abandoning Hansen's traditional way of conducting its business and trying something new and untested. Hansen was a conservative company; coping with this much change made some of the key people who would have to approve Baker's recommendations uneasy. But the resolution would resolve nothing unless it could be sold to Hansen's top management.

Baker and his group listed the ten people who could make or break the new sales project. They listed the wants and needs of each target, as they understood them. Of particular concern was the VP of production, an archconservative for whom the idea of change was poison. What annoyed him the most? Changing production schedules on short notice. Would anything about the new plan help him? Year-long contracts and a stable market would mean that he could plan his own operation more efficiently and avoid having to cope with one crisis after another.

When this benefit was pointed out to him, he was all for the change. He kept calling Baker, wanting to know when the new plan would go into effect, and couldn't they hurry it up? He became a strong champion for Baker and was instrumental in getting the new sales plan adopted. Good salesmanship is getting your customers to see that buying your product is in their own best interests. Self-interest is a powerful motivator. What will appeal to your target and make him want to help you? When you have found that magic key, you have found the way to get your recommendations accepted.

What mode of thinking lets you find this magic key? Intuitive thinking and your best judgment, the product of many years of experience, are the best tools for discovering what will catch the interest of your target. Gut feelings are your best guide. You and your work group have spent your lives learning about people and why they do things the way they do. Listen to what you know. If you think together about it, you can come up with a message that will intrigue and challenge the people who can help get your resolution implemented.

Using the Report to Best Advantage: The Cover Memo

A full report contains a lot of information. Figure 15-2 showed the report of Herb Hammond concerning the voids in the rocket body walls. It summarized the significant data that had led to his conclusions. But it wasn't the heart of Hammond's communication to the people he wanted to influence. The main instrument was a one-page cover memo setting out his recommendations and tying them to the best interests of each target. The full report was provided as an information backup.

The VP of contract relations at Brownlee was greatly concerned about the voids problem. Brownlee's $350 million contract with the main producer of the rocket to fabricate the experimental graphite-fiber rocket bodies was in jeopardy because of the voids. Contract relations needed a good argument to ensure the prime contractor that everything was in hand, quality would be maintained or improved, and there would be no delays. If Hammond had merely handed the VP the full report and left its interpretation up to him, Contract Relations might not have recognized how best to use it. But because Hammond and his group spent some time thinking about possible connections, they were able to suggest an avenue the VP might explore. They did it in the cover memo they sent him, a slightly edited version of which is presented in Figure 15-3.

Figure 15-3. Brownlee Engineering cover letter.

June 14, 1996

To: Stanley Waverly, VP, Contract Relations
From: H. Hammond, Manager, rocket project
Subject: Resolution of the rocket wall voids problem

We have developed a complete resolution for the rocket walls voids problem. Estimated cost is less than $3,000, and the time of implementation is 2 weeks.

The problem has been the tearing apart of layers of graphite fabric within the rocket walls. First noticed 5 weeks ago and continuing to the present time, separation has occurred after the graphite shell has been formed, baked, and cooled.

The cause has been demonstrated to be an insufficient deposit of slipcoat material on the mold because of settling of Teflon particles during application, exacerbated by vigorous buffing (which was required by the prime contractor 6 weeks ago). This increased the extraction pressures needed to remove the shell from the mold, thereby tearing the graphite fabric in the least flexible portion of the lower section. The cause has been proven through laboratory simulation of the extraction process, visual inspection of insufficient Teflon deposit immediately before wrapping, and observation of the settling characteristics of Teflon particles in the slipcoat used.

The requirement for resolution of the problem is ensuring that sufficient amounts of Teflon are deposited on the mold to facilitate extraction. Actions to achieve this are continuous agitation of the slipcoat to prevent settling of Teflon particles, reduced buffing, positive measurement of the Teflon deposit prior to wrapping, and a visual control on the amount of Teflon in the solution and on the mold. Our plan for implementing these actions and a complete report of findings are appended.

We think our prime contractor can be assured that the problem has been resolved because its cause is not technically complicated and is easily corrected and because the deposition of Teflon on the mold can be accurately measured before wrapping to provide a comprehensive quality control. We will be pleased to discuss this resolution with you at your convenience.

An ideal cover memo makes five key points, all on one page. More than that is unnecessary. The details are in the complete report, and the reader can look them up to answer any questions the letter raises. The key points that should be in every cover letter are these:

1. *Problem:* A summary description of the problem, with just enough detail to give a complete picture of what is wrong.

2. *Cause and proof:* A complete statement of the cause, leaving the details for the main report. Enough is described to allow the reader to understand the cause and its proof.

3. *Requirements for resolution:* The things that have to be repaired, improved, corrected, or avoided in order to achieve a complete resolution, with only a few details.

4. *Actions:* A summary of the major actions needed to meet the requirements, with details of the plan left to the full report.

5. *Specific message to the target:* The message directed at meeting the target's interests in general terms, with only enough details to orient the target toward the connection of the finding with his interests, the actual crafting of which is left up to the target.

The message to the target is general, with a bit of what might be called "spin" in politics. Hammond hinted that "vigorous buffing" contributed to the problem and that the prime contractor had instituted the requirement shortly before the trouble started. He also indicated the basic graphite-fiber technology was sound. Hammond didn't tell the VP what to say, but he offered to provide more information if desired. With this background, the VP was able to assure the prime contractor in a way that cleared Brownlee and smoothed things over.

In the Brownlee case, there were five key people to convince, so Hammond wrote five cover memos. The first four paragraphs were the same in each. Only the final paragraphs, aimed specifically at each target, were different. In the real case, Hammond scored five bull's-eyes. He had a follow-up meeting with each key person, in which he enlarged on the cover memo and answered questions. The meetings averaged thirty minutes in length and left each target convinced that Hammond's recommendations were sound and in the target's own best interest. Approval was quickly given and the actions successfully implemented.

Imagine the outcome had Hammond written a report without providing a framework to hold and organize his data. His letter would have been fifteen pages long and taken a day to write. It wouldn't have been as effective as a one-page cover memo with a three-page backup. You've seen reports that tried to include everything. They don't get read or aren't understood. Nothing beats a clear, one-page report.

Reward and Motivation

Collaboration is a voluntary act. You cannot force someone to collaborate with you, because collaboration is freely sharing what you know and think with someone else to achieve a common goal. You can force someone to sit in a meeting with you, but just being there doesn't constitute collaborating. If you want collaboration to continue, you have to reward those who are willing to work with you and share their expertise. You ensure that collaboration will occur by the way you reward and motivate your people.

Reward and motivation are too important to treat in just a few paragraphs, so Chapter 16 is devoted entirely to them. But reward is closely tied to the report you make, so it must be mentioned here as well. Management beyond the ordinary is not complete until you have rewarded and motivated your colleagues and all those who have contributed to your recommendations.

One of the most rewarding things you can do is to let all the people who have contributed to the resolution see and touch the product of their efforts. Send each person a draft copy of your report and ask if there are any suggestions before you finalize the report. This tells your contributors that their ideas are important and gives them pride of authorship. "I helped do that," they'll say, and they'll show the report to their colleagues and brag a bit. They're behind you 100 percent, and they like you better now than they did before. And if they have suggestions or spot errors, you have time to make changes before the report becomes final.

Building the Institutional Memory

People join and leave organizations all the time, taking what they know with them. Perhaps Hammond will be promoted to another function and his group scattered to other projects. Perhaps a similar problem will arise and have to be analyzed once more from the beginning. Or perhaps a legal question will come up, making it important to be able to say just what was done on June 14, 1996, on the rocket project. Who will be able to say what was found and what actions were taken? The memory of the voids problem will have faded, and the details will have been lost.

In the old days, people stayed with an organization for years or a lifetime. But now job mobility is the rule, and what has been learned by the organization is often forgotten in a surprisingly short time. Every organization needs a database so that it can retain what it has learned from hard experience. Otherwise, it is losing one of its most important resources.

A cross-referenced computer file of Problem Resolution Reports is one way to ensure that vital experience will not be lost. "Keeping track of problems and their solutions is one of our biggest failings," says an executive in an aerospace company. "We can't remember what we know, and that can be costly." Every organization needs an institutional memory. A database of problems, causes, and actions provides a body of experience to refer to and learn from. It is easy to create, since your formatted report is the ideal entry for your archive.

HOW TO DO IT

You must report the resolution you and your work group have crafted in the most effective way you can, or nothing will happen. Follow the logical format you used in your analysis so that your audience will understand your conclusions the same way you and your colleagues do; then identify the people who are vital to the acceptance and implementation of your resolution as targets and direct your report specifically to them. To accomplish this, you need to follow these steps:

1. *Set the task.*
   "Our task now is to report our recommendations so that others will accept and support them."
   This tells your work group that the task is to report your recommendations so that your audience will understand and buy into them. Clarity, brevity, and compatibility with the needs of your readers are your guides.

2. *Complete the Problem Resolution Report.*
   "Fill in and complete the Problem Resolution Report."
   Someone is assigned to fill in and complete the Problem Resolution Report, which draws together the logic and information used in the analysis.
   "Is it clear, concise, and accurate?"
   Have the members of your working group read it and agree that it represents your analysis of the problem.

3. *Identify key people as targets.*
   "Who are the people who will be most influential in gaining acceptance and implementation of our recommendations?"
   Identify the people who can best help you gain approval and implementation of your recommendations.
   "Who wants to see the problem resolved and will gain from it?"
   Identify the people who are directly involved and who will personally benefit from having the problem resolved.
   "Who has the power to change and shake things up with respect to this problem?"
   Identify the power people with respect to this problem, people who can bring about change and want to improve things.

4. *Identify the interests and problems of target individuals.*
"What interests, goals, special concerns, or special problems of each of these target individuals might our recommendations affect in a positive way?"
Encourage your people to use intuitive thinking about target individuals to find answers to the "What's in it for me?" question. Discuss and identify the most powerful motivators.

5. *Compose a cover memo for each target individual.*
"Our task now is to summarize our findings so that our targets will understand our conclusions in the same way we do."
Summarize your findings under these five headings in a one-page, nontechnical letter:
   1. *Problem:* What's wrong that needs to be made right
   2. *Cause and proof:* What the cause is and how you know for sure
   3. *Requirements for a resolution:* What needs to be corrected or improved in order to resolve the problem
   4. *Actions:* What actions are recommended
   5. *Specific message to the target:* What you say to the target to get his or her attention and support
"What message would intrigue and get the cooperation and support of this target person?"
Have your colleagues draw on their personal knowledge of the target and their gut feelings about what would get him or her to support your resolution.

6. *Distribute the report to all who should know.*
"Who should get our recommendations?"
Distribute your recommendations to all who should know about them, from top management and your target individuals to those who will be affected by the actions, as well as to your resource group and working group members.

7. *Reward involvement in management beyond the ordinary.*
"What is the best way to reward all those who were involved?"
Reward all those who contributed and give credit to everyone who had a part in reaching this resolution.
Assign responsibility for rewarding actions.

8. *Enter the complete report in the organizational database.*
"Our final job is to file our report so that it won't get lost."
Place the complete Problem Resolution Report in a cross-referenced database so that it can be recovered when needed.

Summary

In Task 10, you ask your co-workers, "How can we report our resolution to have the greatest impact possible?" To do this, set out the logic and the data supporting your analysis so that your audience will understand them and be led to the same conclusions you have reached, and target those who can help you the most and communicate directly with them. You need to take these steps:

1. Set the task.
2. Complete the Problem Resolution Report.
3. Identify key people as targets.
4. Identify the interests and problems of target individuals.
5. Compose a cover memo for each target individual.
6. Distribute the report to all who should know.
7. Reward involvement in management beyond the ordinary.
8. Enter the complete report in an organizational database.

There are two more matters to discuss. The first is how to reward and motivate your people so that they are ready to collaborate with you in resolving the next problem that comes your way. The second is how to install the processes of managing beyond the ordinary in your organization so that the ten tasks are always completed, at every level, with every complex problem that confronts you. These topics will be covered in Chapters 16 and 17.

SECTION THREE

Completing the Process

16

How to Motivate
for Collaboration

Once, people collaborated because they had to. The problems
they faced were so demanding, and their resources so limited,
that it was obvious that everyone had to work together to survive. People lived in small groups, and everyone was known and
visible to everyone else. Everyone had much the same kind of
tools and clothes, ate the same kind of food, and knew and believed much the same things. No one person had much advantage over another except in physical capability. So they talked
together, pooled their knowledge, and came to agreement on
how they would live. Whatever problems came along, they
needed each other and stuck together because they had to. The
choice was to collaborate for the common good or to go under.

With the advent of agriculture and the domestication of animals, which occurred perhaps ten thousand years ago, the opportunity came for some people to obtain surplus food and
resources, and ambitious individuals took advantage of this
opening. They accumulated wealth and, with it, power. Those
few with power could give orders to the many who had none. If
you were a have-not, you did as you were told, hoping your lot
would be easier if you went along with those who had. Those
with power set the directions for others to follow and became
the first leaders and entrepreneurs.

This arrangement continued for centuries. Raids on neigh-
boring groups provided bodies for the labor pool. As projects

became larger and more complex, supervisors and then managers appeared. Authority was top-down, and there were no quality circles or suggestion boxes. If you supplied the muscle, you weren't expected to have any ideas and probably didn't have time to generate any. Collaboration persisted, however, in family and community projects and at times when people had to help each other because there was no other way.

Recent findings in evolutionary psychology have documented a strong predisposition in humans to cooperate and work together to accomplish a common purpose.[1] However, it is also in our genes to act in our own personal interest to get ahead. For thousands of years, these forces have existed side by side. Sometimes they have been in conflict but usually they were not, each being used when appropriate.

Today, the world of work has come full circle. The problems we now face are so complex that no one person can be sure of having all the answers, no matter how much power she has. Once again, we need to depend on each other, to pool our best knowledge and ideas to develop resolutions to our problems. We desperately need more collaboration.

There is, however, one outstanding difference. It is not obvious to everyone that we must collaborate in order to survive. People have to be convinced that collaboration is the best and necessary way to behave. This is hard because the exercise of power is flattering, pleasant, and addictive.

Collaboration is a gift from your workers to you. If you want to manage beyond the ordinary, you have to motivate people to *want* to work with you to resolve problems. You can't succeed any other way.

What Motivates Your Workers?

Self-interest is a great motivator of people. If you can show your workers how they will benefit by collaborating on resolving a problem, they will invest the extra thought and energy. If you make it clear to them how their participation will give them a direct benefit, they will work with you. So the first thing you need to know is: What specific things motivate your staff? The answer is obvious: the belief that their personal world will be better in some important respect if they do. When you can combine the tendency of people to collaborate with their instinct to look out for their own interests, you will have a mighty engine for getting things done.

Kenneth Kovach, of George Mason University, conducted a study to find which personal motivational factors were considered most important by employees.[2] He found that they ranked *interesting work* first in a list of ten motivators, followed by *appreciation by management* and *being well-informed*. Then came *job security* and *compensation*.

Sound familiar? These are the same benefits your workers receive from managing beyond the ordinary. Look at those benefits again. When people collaborate, they get to do something creative beyond the routine confines of their jobs. That makes the work interesting for them. They have a chance to demonstrate what they know and to be recognized by management for their knowledge and abilities. They get to see more of what is going on in the organization. Because they are allowed to provide important information and insight, they become worth more to the organization and more secure in their jobs. And because they are worth more, they get more of the good things we all like to have.

The act of collaborating is largely self-motivating. When your workers collaborate with you, together you create the conditions they value most highly. If you make sure they are given the leadership, freedom, and support that collaboration requires, they will find reward by contributing their skills and knowledge. The more collaborating a well-informed person does, within reason, the more that person wants to collaborate again in the future.

What about motivation for the manager? The same study found that managers ranked *compensation* as their top motivational factor, followed by *job security* and *growth opportunities*, with *working conditions* coming in fourth. If you encourage collaboration and manage beyond the oridnary, you will be worth more to your organization because you will produce more and better and will be eligible for bonuses, promotions, etc. As a result, your job security will be enhanced. When top management looks for someone to head up the next big project, the fact that you can get your people to work with you will be noted. And having people working with you, instead of against you, makes life much more pleasant.

You can guarantee that you and your workers will be motivated only if your collaboration succeeds. If it does, you will have created a true everybody-wins, nobody-loses situation and will have gotten better problem resolutions in addition. So do what it takes to make it succeed.

Making Sure That Your Collaboration Will Be Successful

Your collaboration will succeed if the people you select to work with you want it to succeed. And that depends, ultimately, on your ability to motivate them by leading them through each of the tasks of managing beyond the ordinary. If you do a complete job of it, they will know that the proposed resolution is good and gain satisfaction from being a part of it. Each task will be rewarding for them.

When you explore the situation with them, they feel included and part of something important. When you ask them to help you clarify the purpose of the activity you are concerned with, they feel that they are dealing with fundamental and important matters. When you ask them to collaborate with you, they feel that they are trusted, that their ideas are worth listening to, and that their expertise is valued. Every task makes them feel more worthwhile and less a nameless unit filling a job slot; every task makes them more committed to you and to making a success of the resolution.

Motivating your workers to collaborate means treating them as partners who can *think*. It means *listening* to them and using their ideas, letting them share in the feeling of accomplishment that comes when a near-ideal resolution is created, accepted, and implemented, and seeing that they get full credit for their contributions. If you do these things, your collaboration will succeed.

The collaboration process creates its own reward and motivation to a large extent, but this is not automatic, and it won't happen by itself. You can lead your work group by asking questions; asking good questions gets them thinking about the right issues in the right way, and gives them permission to formulate their own opinions from facts, knowledge, experience, and imagination. Then you give them time to think and discuss. If you do these things, they will learn to work and think together and will look for the next opportunity to do it again. Their attitudes toward problems will change, and they will see it as their responsibility to find a resolution, not as someone else's.

Our experience has convinced us that the best motivation comes from inside the person, not from outside. In organizations where managers collaborate with their staffs and stress working together, the atmosphere is very different from that in places where strict hierarchies prevail. People in collaborative organizations have an increased concern for quality and for the well-being of the organization. They search for problems and aggressively find resolutions for them, at all levels. Collaboration becomes a way of life. In 1989, Toyota received 1,960,786 suggestions for improvement from its employees around the world, for an average of more than thirty-four suggestions *per employee* for the year. The company implemented 97 percent of these, or 1,901,962 real resolutions to real problems, large and small.[3] Compare this with a factory in the same industry where collaboration was not the way of life: management received only sixteen suggestions from its 1,700 employees for the same year, only nine of which were implemented.[4]

Managers have to create an environment that fosters collaboration. In the plant that generated only sixteen suggestions in a year, nobody cared much whether problems were resolved, and management didn't encourage people to think, so nothing much got done. If you give orders and wait for them to be carried out, you'll get one thing. If you work together with your colleagues, lead them and motivate them to use their own intelligence to find better resolutions, you'll get something else. And we say the something else is a whole lot better. Asking questions to stimulate collaboration is something you can do any time you want to, in any place, under any conditions. It is entirely up to you.

Causes of Collaborative Failures

Attempts at collaboration sometimes fail, and people aren't motivated to think and work together. This result is usually caused
by a failure of leadership. Someone has to identify the problem
and say that collaboration in resolving it is the objective. Someone has to select good resource people, point out that collaboration is in everyone's best interest, and show why. Someone has
to ask questions that will focus people's attention on the problem. Someone has to listen to the ideas that are contributed. If
there is no leadership, people don't know what to do, what
they're supposed to accomplish, or whether anyone is interested
in what they think. The effort can break down into confusion
and resentment, leading people to feel that they have been used
once again by a management that doesn't care enough to tell
them what is going on or to take them seriously.

Lack of trust is another cause of failure. If people are going
to work together, they have to trust one another. If they feel that
management is playing a game, doesn't really intend to share
information and ideas, and is interested only in getting more
without giving anything in return, they will be suspicious and
withhold their ideas. The worst thing you can do is tell them
only part of the story. They will suspect you of having a secret
agenda and of manipulating them for your own ends. Trust will
go out the window, and it will occur to them that their best
interest probably lies in not saying or doing anything; the opportunity for collaboration will simply vanish. If you take people
into your confidence and share ideas with them, ask them questions and listen to their answers, they'll feel they're a part of the
action and will want to help.

Another thing that kills collaboration is playing status
games, reminding people that you are a manager and they are
lower in the scheme of things. You may make more money than
they do and have a reserved parking space, but if you want them
to collaborate with you, you have to treat them as equals in their
knowledge of the problem—because they know things you
don't, which is why you need them and their experience and
judgment. Hierarchy and job titles are beside the point in the

resolution of a problem. Together you and your work group will get to the answer, but not if you are up here and they are down there.

Finally, people will not continue to contribute unless they sense that they are getting somewhere. You must show them the results of their efforts. When a person offers an idea, acknowledge the idea so that the person knows that you are listening and can feel satisfaction at having contributed something. Praise people for their creativity and efforts. Managers have the reputation of saying something only when things go wrong and seldom commenting when they go well. That doesn't motivate your people to collaborate, so turn your behavior around and exploit every opportunity you get to say something positive. It is almost impossible to give too much credit to your colleagues.

Getting the Attention of Top Management

As a manager, you are the mouthpiece for your group. You have to make your group's accomplishments visible to others in management in order to make sure that your group gets credit for the good things it does. If you don't do this, nobody else will, and the rest of the people in your organization won't even know your group exists. It's easy to say nothing and let top management think you solved the problem all by yourself, not exactly stealing the credit but getting it because you failed to mention your co-workers as the ones who made it happen. You receive the credit by default, and they receive nothing through your silence. The word will get around, however, and your efforts at collaboration next time will backfire.

You can give your co-workers credit in several ways. You can be a spokesperson for them; when you report progress in resolving a problem, say, "Joe Wilson, Mamie Baldridge, and Chester Stuart found and proved the cause on this problem." Not "I," which would suggest that you did it by yourself, or "my people," which would imply a herd of robots at work somewhere. When you use names, you bring to management's attention the real people out there who are working for the interests of the organization.

You also bring attention to what your co-workers do by passing on anecdotes about their good work. Top managers need to know what is being accomplished in their organizations and are hungry for examples they can relate to others to show how progressive and well informed they are. One of the authors made a presentation to an audience of CEOs. He told of a situation in which a supervisor and three repairmen went beyond the ordinary to resolve a problem that had plagued the organization for years. When he finished, a man in the audience stood up and said, "That's my company, and I'm the CEO of it. I have to come to a conference like this to find out what some of my people are doing. That's not right. When I go back, I'm going to shake the hands of those four people, and I'm going to find out why I don't hear first off when someone does something good like that."

Executives like to tell good things about their companies, just as parents like to tell good things about their kids. That CEO would have been proud to tell his peers about the intiative and the imagination of his people, had he known about them, because that would have reflected favorably on him and the kind of heads-up organization he directed. Give him the ammunition to do just that. And think about this for a moment: It also reflects well upon you when you can pass on such an anecdote. Without saying so, you are giving proof that you are a manager who goes beyond the ordinary when you lead your subordinates into doing more than the routine things they were hired to do. You can't lose by letting others know how capable your co-workers are.

You can also bring the accomplishments of your subordinates to top management's attention by helping to set up a formal reward system. You might, for example, require that whenever a report of a problem resolution is given, the names of all participants be recorded and included or that instances of outstanding participation be noted in the individual's personnel file and go to those who need to know about good performance. This may make a difference at promotion and bonus-award time. It is in the best interests of the organization that the best people be identified and given added responsibility. If there is no way these people can be recognized, there is no way the organization can know who shows unusual promise and should be developed.

Remember Gene Summers in Chapter 5, the general manager who turned around the agricultural product processing plant? He set up a formal system of communication and reward. When an individual or group came up with a resolution, he was informed about it and visited the site, where he saw and heard about the resolution for himself, directly from the people involved. He made it a routine to write short notes to everyone who contributed to a resolution. He had lunch with a different group of his subordinates each week to hear their problems and to share information. His reward system lifted that plant out of the swamps and give it new life. When he saw one of his notes framed above a mechanic's workbench, he knew the plant had turned the corner. If he hadn't made a particular point of rewarding his workers, motivating them to do better and building pride in the operation, that plant would have died. Gene Summers led his workers to make it successful. Any other manager can do the same thing.

A System of Motivation and Reward

A motivation and reward system depends on having a system for measuring achievement. Did what you wanted to happen in fact occur? If you don't know whether or not it happened, you can't provide either motivation or reward. You have to define what you want to happen, determine what evidence you will accept as proof that it did or did not happen, and then provide an appropriate means of collecting and communicating the information.

1. *Define what you want to happen.* What change or new behavior is desired? Too often, general results, such as "profitability" or "growth of the business," are suggested. These are global effects and are hard to relate to the actions of your workers. To get more useful answers, go to those in top management who will be evaluating the success of your efforts. Ask them what they want to have happen. "What changes or improvements do

you want to see?" Get it in their words. Here are some measures of improvement that some of our client managers have said would be important to them in specific problems:

- Reduced turnover of assembly-line workers
- Less downtime on Line One
- Faster response to customer complaints
- More customers satisfied with the service they receive
- Quicker resolution of problems, with everybody agreeing with the actions recommended

Be prepared for some surprises. The results desired often are not expressed in dollars and may not be what you assume would be important to the person evaluating your resolution. Whatever the measure is, be sure you know how to define it in the terms of the person who will do the judging.

2. *Define what constitutes evidence of success.* Then ask, "What would you accept as evidence that this change did occur?" This is as important to know as the goal itself. What countable units will be taken as valid and relevant? For the client who named "reduced turnover of assembly-line workers" as the most important measure, the evidence was "the number of quits, the number of fires, and how long each worker had been on the job before leaving." For the measure "faster response to customer complaints," the evidence of change was "hours from receipt of complaint to a satisfactory response to whomever complained." For "quicker resolution of problems, with everybody agreeing with the actions recommended," the evidence was "how long it takes to solve the problem and the number of people disagreeing with the actions taken."

A baseline or standard against which to compare change is necessary to answer the question "Compared to what?" For turnover, the standard was the rate for the previous six-month period; for complaints, it was the actual response times for a sample of cases. You may have to document how quickly problems were handled in the past and how satisfied people were with the resolutions to put together a standard. For all measures, however, you can find some value against which to say, "It was that before, and it's this now."

You will have to devise a way of gathering the specific data you need. It usually isn't hard, once you know what you need to count. Turnover rates are easy, and so is downtime. A complaint response log will collect what you need to know about speed of handling, and a few phone calls will tell you how well they are now being handled. You don't need an elaborate study to get useful results information. You can say, "Turnover rates were this high before, and now they have been reduced by 61 percent. Quits have been cut in half, firings have been reduced by 10 percent, and people stay on the line twice as long before moving." With this information, you can easily figure the dollar savings if you want to.

3. *Provide a means of collecting and communicating the information.* You need to work out a way of getting the results to whomever requested or will use it. When you ask what evidence of change or improvement will be accepted, also ask, "How do you want to get word of these results?" Let the person defining the results tell you what kind of communication would be most convenient. That way, the recipient of the report has ownership in it because he helped design it, and your report will be expected and will have interest and meaning for the recipient. Don't be surprised if you are asked to "drop by and tell me so that I can ask any questions I might have." The offer to measure and report the results of a problem resolution is so unusual that it will attract special attention. Trade on it. It provides an important channel to use in making visible your subordinates' contributions to the organization—and your performance as a manager. Your organization needs this kind of information, and it is important for you to help provide it.

Your subordinates need it as well. If together you have gone to the trouble of resolving a problem, others should hear what the results are. Any reports of appreciation you can take back to your workers will be motivating. Good results encourage people to produce even better results next time.

If you set up a motivation and reward system whenever you can, you will make your work group want to help you next time. It will make the group members think of you as a partner, not just as another manager who doesn't know who they are or what they are capable of doing.

If this seems too much extra work for you, think of the benefit you'll gain from it. Then think how you can delegate most of the work, such as setting up measures and collecting data, to someone else. If you tell them what you want and how to go about it, others can do this for you. In time, this will become an automatic part of resolving every problem.

HOW TO DO IT

You have to motivate people if you expect them to want to collaborate with you. That means helping them receive benefits from the collaboration that are in their own best interests. To do that, you must know what those interests are and then make it happen. To accomplish this, follow these steps:

1. *Set the task for yourself.*
   "My task is to provide enough benefit from collaboration that my subordinates will want to work with me."
   Motivation is your job and no one else's. Your task is to make cooperation and collaboration worth people's time so that they will want to work with you to find the best resolution possible.

2. *Serve the needs of those who collaborate with you.*
   You need to identify and meet the needs of those whom you want to collaborate with you.
   "What can I do to make collaboration interesting work for them?"
   Broaden their knowledge of what is going on, challenge their imaginations, get them to contribute their experience. Give them the freedom to think through the problem and put forward their own ideas.
   "What can I do to show appreciation for their knowledge, experience, judgment, and imagination?"
   Listen and react to their contributions, help them get their ideas out, use and build on their ideas, give individual credit, and avoid being critical. Tell others of their good work, and show respect for them every way you can.

"What can I do to make sure they are kept well informed?"
State your goals and purpose, fill them in on problem information, don't hold back any part of the story, and summarize often. Use any means to keep them informed of what is going on.

"What can I do to further ensure their job security?"
Give individuals credit by name, enter credit in their records, talk up their capabilities and contributions, and let others know how valuable they are.

"What can I do to increase their compensation?"
Enter credit for their participation in the records, and remember their efforts for bonus or other purposes. Stand up for them, and don't let their good work be forgotten or overlooked. Make the importance of their collaboration visible to management and to others who may influence their compensation and job futures.

"What else can I do to make my subordinates want to work with me?"
Watch to see what else they value highly that might be used to spur their collaboration. Look for opportunities to say "Thank you" and "Your ideas helped a lot." You can't acknowledge people's good efforts too often.

3. *Establish a results measurement system.*
If you don't measure the results of your collaboration, nobody will ever know what good work you and your co-workers have done.

"What results do you want to achieve?"
Ask whomever will evaluate your project what results she wants, and make sure you get these results in those terms.

"What evidence of results will be accepted?"
Find out what measures are important and what management will accept as evidence of improvement.

"What baseline can we use for comparison?"
Find out what the performance was before, in practical terms, so that you can compare it against the performance after.

Gather the specific data you need.
Get the specific answers you need and nothing more. If you know precisely what you want to know, you can have someone else get the information for you.

"How do you want to get word of these results?"
Ask whomever will evaluate your project how she wants to get the results so that the information will be presented to her the way she likes and finds convenient.

4. *Communicate the results of your problem resolution.*

Keep your co-workers informed of what has happened.
Your colleagues are more interested in the results of their efforts than anyone else, so let them know fully and at once what's going on.

Keep top managers informed.
They need to know what progress is being made so that they can understand what is going on and take this into consideration when making other decisions.

Keep your peers and colleagues informed.
They need to know what changes are being made so that they can work with you and your work group and have confidence in what you do.

Summary

You can motivate your subordinates so that they will want to collaborate with you in finding the best possible resolution by doing these things:

- Showing them that resolving the problem is in their best interest
- Making collaboration interesting for them
- Showing appreciation for what they know and what they can do
- Sharing information to keep them well informed
- Enhancing their job security as much as possible
- Improving their compensation and reward as much as possible
- Looking for any other ways to motivate and reward them

To set up a system to track the effects of your resolution and to get that information to all who need and can use it, it's necessary to:

- Determine the results desired
- Determine what evidence of improvement is acceptable
- Establish a baseline for comparison

- Arrange for the collection of specific data
- Determine how information about results should be communicated

There is only one further matter to consider: how to install these techniques and procedures on the job so that they can help you and your co-workers manage beyond the ordinary tomorrow and every day after that.

Notes

1. Robert Wright, *The Moral Animal* (New York: Pantheon Books, 1994).
2. Kenneth Kovach, As paraphrased in *Boardroom Reports,* October 15, 1994.
3. Ian Winfield, *Japan Management Review* 2, no. 2 (1994).
4. Personal communication, Plant Manager to Charles Kepner, Detroit, 1993.

17

How to Install and Maintain Collaboration

You have thought about managing beyond the ordinary and want to get your co-workers to collaborate with you on a problem, but you are not sure how to go about it. This chapter tells you all you need to know.

To enlist the support of your co-workers, you must be convinced that collaboration is a desirable way of operating, you must commit to providing the leadership required, and you must support the effort throughout. If you do these things and complete the ten tasks described in Chapter 3, you will succeed at managing beyond the ordinary. If you aren't convinced, committed, and willing to support the effort to the end, it won't work. Nobody can be insincere and succeed at collaboration. Your co-workers will see through any pretense. And if you can't enlist your co-workers to help you, you won't be able to get anything done.

You have to accomplish these three things to achieve successful collaboration:

1. Introduce the idea of collaboration and convince your co-workers that you need and will use their help
2. Install the procedures for accomplishing the ten tasks and do any necessary training or coaching so that people know what to do
3. Support collaboration until the problem has been re-

solved and you and your colleagues have framed your recommendations for action.

The Three Levels of Application

There are three levels of application for the ideas of collaboration and managing beyond the ordinary. The first, and the simplest, is to use the ideas as an individual, attacking one problem at a time and using the procedures as a personal management tool. At this level, you work with your colleagues to deal with a problem that affects you all, leading them by asking questions that get them thinking in the directions you want them to go, rather than by telling them what to do. They discover the answers and create the best possible resolution with you from their funds of knowledge and expertise.

The second level of application involves an organizational unit, such as a section, department, branch, or office. Several managers form a coalition and, acting as a group of individuals, make full use of what their subordinates know. Problems are resolved, and, over time, collaboration becomes a part of the unit's culture because it works and brings satisfaction to those who participate.

At the third level of application, an organization formally installs and maintains a program of collaboration and managing beyond the ordinary as a policy. The organization says, "We want these ideas and procedures to become a way of life with our support." The organization establishes a program of training in collaboration and its application because it believes collaboration will improve quality and save money. It is an official effort to improve efficiency and is strongly supported.

Excellent results can be obtained at any of the three levels. Which level you choose will be determined by what you want to accomplish. You can start with an individual effort, extend it to an organizational unit, and then to an official, organization-wide program. Or you can start at the unit level or with a full organizational program. These are different packages of the same thing: managing beyond the ordinary through collaboration with your co-workers.

Level 1: The Individual

If you use these procedures as an individual, your first task will be to pick an appropriate problem to resolve. The problem should be complex enough to require the skills and insights of a number of people and should be one about which a reasonable amount of information is available. It should also be one of concern to and within the knowledge of the people around you. It should also lie within your area of responsibility so that you don't come up against barriers of hierarchy and authority that stop you before you get started.

When you have identified your problem, select one or two people to form a working group with you. Tell them what you are going to do and why. Get them copies of this book to act as a reference manual so that they will know what you are talking about. Suggest that they mark it up and make notes as you go along. Better yet, you might all take part together in an application workshop or seminar to learn the procedures and how to use them on the job. (More will be said about training later in this chapter.)

Decide what your real purpose is and who can give you the ideas and information you will need to achieve it. Invite these people to join you, explaining to them what you are going to do and how they can benefit from it. Start with only a few resource people, remembering that you can add others as the need for them and their ideas becomes apparent.

Ask questions and lead the working group through the tasks that need to be completed. You will need to explain the process to them as you go along. When they understand each task and the reason for your questions, it will all make sense, and they will cooperate with you, but you may have to do a little coaching along the way. Your co-workers will collaborate with you to get the procedures straight as well as to resolve the problem itself.

A manager in a large state government agency called one of his subordinates into his office, handed her a draft version of this book, and said, "Read this, and then pick out the location of our next new branch office." (The agency needed to open another branch in a suburban area that had grown rapidly.) The manager gave his subordinate no further help, just offered the material. She read the text, collected a working group, drew in resource people, and selected a location that later turned out to be excellent. She and her working group must have had some anxious moments, but they were successful. We don't recommend this minimal, do-or-die approach, but it worked. If you lead your group by questioning and a bit of coaching, you will make the experience easy and enjoyable.

You will need to motivate and reward your working group as you go along. You and your working group will keep your resource people on track and collect and organize the information they contribute. You will ask questions and lead people to the best recommendations they can make. In the end, a member of your working group can pull it all together in a report. The entire process can be carried out successfully by you as an individual, in low profile, with no drums, bells, or whistles. Because of this, it is a riskfree venture that can only produce good. You can successfully manage beyond the ordinary on your own, just as many others have.

Level 2: The Organizational Unit

An organizational unit, such as a department, office, or branch, may decide to install collaboration and management beyond the ordinary. To do so, the head and the managers of the unit band together to act individually but in coordination in a low-key, local management improvement effort. Their purpose is to make collaboration a way of doing business within their unit, although not necessarily within the rest of the organization.

The unit staff meeting is a good place for such an effort to start. The head of the unit introduces the idea, and the unit's managers agree they want to encourage collaboration. They discuss what they will need to do and commit to lead and coach their subordinates as necessary. They agree to support and maintain the effort and to do whatever is required to make it successful.

The problems to be handled are the complex ones that come to the staff meeting in the usual course of events. They are assigned to the managers by the unit head or chosen by the managers themselves. From this point on, the managers act as individuals, working with their subordinates to find the best resolutions possible. They ask questions, lead, coach, and motivate people to collaborate.

When a unit undertakes managing beyond the ordinary, more structure is required for the effort than if it were to be carried out by individual initiative alone. Many organizations have an orientation session for supervisors and others that explains what the managers are up to. The managers often receive formal training in the procedures through seminars and are better able to coach their people as a result. They and their working groups also usually go through a one-day workshop in the application of the procedures, applying them to the kinds of problems they must deal with on the job.

A unit approach is intended to continue over time as the way the unit does business, dealing with one problem after another. Because of its ongoing nature, a unit approach is better able to measure results and develop a program of motivation and reward. The unit head is involved from the beginning and lends support to the effort. It is a local activity, changing unit operational policy but without challenging or affecting the management policies of the organization as a whole, at least at first. Over time, however, the accomplishments of the unit will have an effect on the organization through example.

A department of a large organization took this approach and was recognized as being more innovative and successful than it had been in the past. At an executive meeting, the CEO asked, "What are you people doing down there?" The department head made a short speech outlining the unit's efforts to encourage collaboration and passed on some anecdotes about resolutions it had achieved. The CEO was impressed and suggested that other departments consider doing the same. Before long, an organizationwide program had been established that involved everyone in the company.

Level 3: A Formal Organizational Program

A formal organizational program takes place after top management has decided, as a matter of policy, that collaboration and managing beyond the ordinary should be adopted by everyone and takes actions to see that this occurs. The organization holds orientation sessions on the theory and practice of collaboration, and two-day seminars led by outside training consultants are held for managers and supervisors, giving them instruction on how to use the procedures and apply them on the job. Better yet, the organization may select several senior training persons and have them qualify to lead the seminars in-house. In-house seminar instructors can do an excellent job since they know the problems of the organization, are already on staff, and can act as collaboration consultants to their own colleagues whenever a need for special help arises. They can do much to maximize the returns from the organization's investment.

The organizational approach has some advantages over the individual and the unit methods. When the organization adopts a particular management style as a matter of policy, it sets public expectations for results. Managers know that they are expected to make the new system work. Money and effort have been invested in the system, and they know top management is watching. On the other hand, organizational programs sometimes try to move too fast with too little support, assuming that there is more understanding and commitment on the part of managers than actually exists. If a company tries to do too much, it may produce only superficial results. If managers are truly convinced that collaboration works in their favor and is not just another fad, the organizational approach produces spectacular success. One good result motivates another, and when the entire organization is behind the effort, benefits add up rapidly.

An organizational approach requires good communication to keep everyone informed about the results achieved. This is important because it provides motivation to the participants and to top management, which sponsored the effort. Support must be continuous. The worst thing that can happen is for management to assume that the organizational program is fully established after a few months and requires no further attention. Managing beyond the ordinary demands extra care, thought, and effort— not much, but some, to keep the ideas alive. It must be an ongoing activity, because it is easy for old habits to rise up again and for some managers to lose sight of the good they have gained through collaboration. In the end, success depends on the organization. If collaboration and managing beyond the ordinary are neglected, they will fade from use, for at least some people.

Application Workshops and Seminars

Good training helps bridge the gap between learning new ideas and putting those ideas into practice. One-day application workshops allow managers and other participants to practice using new ideas and procedures to resolve real, on-the-job problems under the leadership of a qualified professional; two- and three-day seminars, led by a qualified outside or specially trained in-house instructor, teach the ideas and procedures in more detail. The purpose of these workshops and seminars is to fine-tune participants' knowledge of the procedures and to take the first steps in applying them to real-life problems; the goal is to make the participants feel confident and ready to use the procedures on the job the next day.

Workshops and seminars can be modified to serve those who use computer software, such as Lotus Notes, in support of collaboration. In a sense, the workshops provide a common program for the participants' mental computers to help them use the software programs in their electronic ones. This is important, for if computer users have data pouring in faster than ever before but no common way of dealing with it, collaboration can be difficult. When they have both a powerful electronic way of gathering and manipulating data and a clear procedure for handling it, they will find their productivity greatly increased.

HOW TO DO IT

If you want managing beyond the ordinary to take hold in your organization, you have to introduce the ideas, install the techniques and procedures, and then support and maintain them. This requires that you do these things:

1. *Set the task.*
   "My task is to introduce the ideas of collaboration, install the necessary techniques and procedures, and support and maintain them so that they work."

This sets out your purpose and reminds you that it's up to you to ask the questions that will lead your working group to think and do what you know will make them more productive.

2. *Obtain commitment that collaboration is the way to go.*
   "Are we all in favor of collaboration?"
   Get conviction and commitment to collaboration and agreement to support the problem resolution process.
   "Are we ready to work together to install collaboration?"
   Get enthusiastic support for collaboration as a way of resolving problems and making decisions.

3. *Decide on the level of application.*
   "Will we do best at the individual, unit, or organizational level of application?"
   Pick the most useful level for your situation and the problems you want to resolve.

4. *Pick an appropriate problem for resolution.*
   "Is it complex, requiring the knowledge of several people?"
   "Is there a reasonable amount of information available?"
   "Is it within the knowledge of my subordinates?"
   "Is it within my sphere of responsibility?"
   If the problem meets these criteria, it should be suitable for resolution through collaboration.

5. *Form your working group.*
   "Who knows something about this situation, has a stake in the problem, is willing to collaborate, and will work with me to resolve it?"
   Pick one or two people who know a good deal about the situation, have a personal stake in it, and with whom you can cooperate to make up your working group. Pick people who can ask questions and are respected by those who will be your resource persons.
   Invite them to join you as your working group.
   Tell them what you are trying to do, why you chose them, and what they will get out of it (motivate!), and ask them to be in your working group. Don't pressure anyone to join. Collaboration must be voluntary.

6. *Get the information out.*
   "What's going on?"
   Ask questions to clarify the problem. Get different views from people who know it firsthand.

Describe the problem as you see it now.
Separate issues, set priorities, get agreement.
Understand where you are, what the situation is, and what is important.

7. *Question your real purpose with regard to this problem.*
"What are we really trying to do here?"
Ask what the purpose is, whether you should clarify it, state a new purpose, or modify it in some way.
Make your best statement of purpose, and agree on it.

8. *Decide who should be involved.*
"What information do we need and who has it?"
Decide what kind of information you need, who will be your resource people, and how you will get them to cooperate.
Invite your resource people to contribute.
Ask them, but don't pressure them. Tell them what they will get out of it (motivate!). Get their commitment to collaborate with you.
Identify and recruit a champion.
Determine who is influential and has something to gain in this situation, and ask for and get that person's commitment to help.

9. *Proceed through the ten tasks in order.*
"What is the problem, and what is not affected?"
Move through the ten tasks, from achieving an in-depth understanding of the problem to communicating for acceptance.

10. *Motivate and reward your people at every opportunity.*
"How can I provide benefit and reward to my people for their collaboration in resolving this problem?"
Ask yourself this question, then follow through and do it. People are motivated to act only after they see how they can benefit.

11. *Support and encourage collaboration.*
"How can I support and encourage collaboration so that it continues to be the best way to deal with complex problems?"
Measure and report results, pass on antecdotes, and talk up its quality, economic, psychological, and morale benefits.
Use it as a serious management tool, and encourage other managers to do the same.
Become known as collaboration's champion. This will mark you as a manager beyond the ordinary.

Summary

You have learned how to install and support collaboration as a necessary step in managing beyond the ordinary. You know how to make it succeed and how to make its results visible. You know you can do it by asking questions and listening to your subordinates and by making them want to work with you to resolve problems. Now all you have to do is do it. Deciding to go ahead is all that remains to be done.

18

You Can Do It

Managing beyond the ordinary is common-sense behavior applied to resolving problems. It is working with other people to get out the best information that exists among all of you and doing the best you can with it. It's allowing others to contribute what they know to the resolution of problems that concern you all and to share in the satisfaction of having made things better.

Managing beyond the ordinary is simply doing a complete job of dealing with a problem and its issues. It is knowing when you are confronted by complexity that you can't easily deal with by yourself and enlisting the aid of those who know things about it that you don't. It is tapping the resources of your organization to get a better resolution to a problem that affects all of you. It is thinking together to find a better way.

But nothing will happen unless you take that first step. There is no reason for you to hesitate; you will always be in control and in a position to see that nothing goes off track. Collaboration is a management tool that serves your needs, as well as bringing fulfillment and satisfaction to others. The time to start is right now, while the ideas are fresh in your mind. If you wait until next week, you may never get around to it. Try it quietly and on your own at first. Convince yourself that it is good for you and your organization; then use it wherever and whenever it seems to fit.

You can do it, and you should. You owe it to yourself to try, because the future lies with those who can manage people working together to get complex things done. When you can enlist the full cooperation of your subordinates, you will be able to accomplish things you couldn't have done before.

Your organization may be realigned and reoriented to better support collaboration,[1] or it may not. Either way, you can put your head together with those of your best-informed co-workers and think collectively to find a more complete resolution to any complex problem that faces you. You can expand tremendously your scope of knowledge and experience simply by asking your sharpest colleagues for their ideas. Then you an integrate their ideas with your own, use them or set them aside depending upon your best judgment, and produce a resolution that incorporates the best thinking of all those involved.

Do it! You can, you know. And you will find this new way of managing worth many times the effort of trying something different. It will change your life and the lives of those around you. None of you will ever be the same again.

Good luck, and good managing!

Note

1. Edward M. Marshall, *Transforming The Way We Work: The Power of the Collaborative Workplace* (New York: AMACOM, 1995).

Bibliography

Caesar, Julius. *The Civil War.* Transl. Jane P. Gardner. New York: Dorset Press, 1985.

Champy, James. *Reengineering Management.* New York: HarperBusiness, 1995.

Decision Pad. Menlo Park, Calif.: Apian Software.

Hammer, Michael, and James Champy. *Reengineering the Corporation.* New York: HarperBusiness, 1993.

Kayser, Thomas A. *Mining Group Gold.* Chicago: Irwin, 1995.

Kovach, Kenneth. *Boardroom Reports,* October 15, 1994.

Marshall, Edward M. *Transforming the Way We Work: The Power of the Collaborative Workplace.* New York: AMACOM, 1995.

McConnell, Malcolm. *Challenger, A Major Malfunction.* New York: Doubleday, 1987.

Pascale, Richard Tanner. *Managing on the Edge.* New York: Simon and Schuster, 1990.

Rogers, William P. *Report to the President by the Presidential Commission on the Space Shuttle Challenger Accident.* Washington, D.C.: Government Printing Office, 1986.

Schrage, Michael. *Shared Minds.* New York: Random House, 1990.

Winfield, Ian. *Japan Management Review,* no. 2, 1994.

Wright, Robert. *The Moral Animal.* New York: Pantheon Books, 1994.

Index